MW01088573

The Hebrew Masoretic Text: Inerrancy Preserved through Divine Providence

Scholar-Skeptics Refuted

by
L. Bednar, D.Min.

**Indiana Fundamental Bible College of the
Grace Bible Baptist Church, New Paris, IN
Dr. Daniel S. Haifley, President and Pastor**

> **Emphasizing translation of the
> Received-Text basis of the KJB
> to give God's true Word to world
> people groups in their languages**

Prologue

Scholars say the content of our standard Hebrew text has varied through centuries of evolution. That's how they explain variance from the Masoretic Text in ancient texts like the Septuagint and targumim translations and some Hebrew Dead-Sea scrolls. Such thinking is typical of modern efforts to make evolution the source of all things, and deny preservation of autograph originals to discredit belief in divine providence. The mere fact that texts related to the Masoretic vary from it in content, doesn't signify change in the Masoretic Text itself. God preserves His Word, for the entire text shows consistent accuracy indicative of inerrancy (illustrated here and elsewhere [a]), indicating each book added has always been so fixed in content, it preserves autograph inerrancy.

The variance observed among some texts has no implications for Masoretic-Text accuracy. It's due to a unique Hebrew-text edition paralleling the standard text late in history and amplifying (advancing or clarifying) partial revelation, mystery or subtlety, largely at passages with veiled references to Christ and the future church. Ancient versions of the right chronology are from the amplified text. In the standard Masoretic, some early topics are amplified by later ones as part of the content: e.g. In Ezk.40-48, old priest/temple types advance to new Millennial-era types, and Ezk.38,39 advance knowledge of Armageddon in Joel 3. And the New Testament amplifies the Old: e.g. Christ's defeat of anti-christ, the false prophet & vast armies at Armageddon in Rev.19: 11-21 further advances Ezk.38,39 comment on the battle. New-Testament amplification clarified veiled matters with finality, so the church understood veiled or partially-veiled topics in the standard Masoretic Text on Christ and topics like the Tribulation, Armageddon & the Millennium. Amplification ended only when New-Testament completion closed the canon at ~100 A.D to fix the content of the standard text of the Bible as a whole forever.

a. *The Case for Preservation of God's Inerrant Word.* WCBS book

2

Now textual scholarship is valuable if it distinguishes truth from error, but modern scholarship often promotes error and discredits truth. This writer's unyielding stand on the Received Text (both the New and Old Testaments), is a result of many years of study revealing the stamp of God's preservation on it, and a lack of this in modern texts. Faith in God must guide scholarship, and the time has come to seek to dispel the hold of humanist scholars on men's minds, and awaken a slumbering world to the treasures of God's true inerrant Word. This task, that will point people to the true God, is both a great privilege and a great duty.

The Nature of this Treatise

The Case for the Preservation of God's Inerrant Word offered evidence of inerrancy of the true New-Testament text, and some for the Old. The Old is complex due to unique text history. Here we elaborate on inerrancy and uniqueness of the Masoretic Text, specifically the Ben Chayyim (Bomberg ed), the basis of the KJB Old Testament and part of the Bible-believer's Received Text.

This book has no contents table, for it must be read through to see all the implications. A few uncommon terms are defined in a glossary at the book closure. Regarding text format, closely related paragraphs are marked by indentation, and less-directly related ones are marked by a skipped space. Text references of more immediate relevance are in footnotes marked by asterisks.

Summary of Findings in Old Testament Studies

The earlier treatise provided evidence of divine dictation and guidance of the Masoretic Text, accounting for the indicated inerrancy. Further observations on the unique textual nature and history of this inerrant text are summarized below.

1. Inspiration includes amplifying (advancing/clarifying) of one Old-Testament passage by another, or by the New Testament. Amplification of Samuel and Kings by Chronicles is a primary example of the type contained within the Old Testament.

2. Amplification is progressive revelation originating, in part, in some unique, anonymous, canonical margin notes (Heb. *qere*) added before the Old-Testament canon closed. Such qere can be verified as canonical, as in the case of some Samuel/Kings qere that appear in the <u>texts</u> of Masoretic Chronicles. Most qere are non-canonical notes added by the Masoretes in the Middle Ages.

3. Amplification occurs in texts of Masoretic books of prophets, as in Ezk.ch.40-48 where priesthood and temple types of 1 Kings and 2 Chronicles advance to future Millennial-era types.

A unique amplification source created text variety wrongly attributed to evolution by scholars, a Masoretic-Text edition by Ezra et al, paralleling the standard text late in pre-church history. This text and its original Septuagint translation amplified veiled Masoretic-Text Christology in the 1st-century A.D. before the permanent New Testament appeared, explaining why the church of the 1st century revered the Septuagint Old-Testament version.

4. Confusion over two somewhat different text-types in standard 2nd-1st century B.C temple manuscripts would be due mainly to the amplified Hebrew text (unadvertised to avoid controversy).

5. The amplified Hebrew text and its translations were later made obsolete by corruption, as necessary to avoid competition with the Masoretic. But the amplified Hebrew is still visible in Dead-Sea scrolls said to be of Septuagint character. It's visible even in extremely-corrupt Vaticanus/Sinaiticus Septuagint texts of little value otherwise. It's presence at Psalm 22:16 in a few standard Masoretic-Text manuscripts and qere reveals its interim validity.

6. Amplification is preserved in its final destination, Received-Text New and Old Testaments and authorized translations of them for ministry in the church, the final estate of God's people.

7. There is no reason to doubt a standard Hebrew text of fixed content throughout text history, amplification explaining variance in other texts and refuting theory on an evolving changing text.

Unique Distinctions of the Inerrant Masoretic Text Preserved in the KJB

Topic A. Even Margin Notes Reveal God's Hand

Margin notes (Heb. *qere*) comment on text (Heb. *ketiv*) language and vocalization.[*] Qere vowels are assigned to ketiv consonants and pronounced in oral readings. Qere can seem to correct the text, but study indicates they amplify (advance/clarify) it. Middle-Ages Masorete qere are just new-language adaptation, but some very ancient anonymous qere are canonical, advancing inerrancy.

Most Masorete qere address ketiv terms said to be error, but they are plentiful, and meticulous text care by the Masoretes virtually eliminated error. Qere really up-date spelling convention, which isn't error correction, but clarification ensuring true interpretation. Some Masorete qere offer valid alternative language.

Some anonymous qere reflect the divine hand and so would precede canon closing. They relate to the progressive way God revealed His Word over the centuries, amplifying early subtle, mysterious or partial-revelation ketiv. Some Samuel/Kings qere contribute to Chronicles ketiv, so canonical Chronicles verify the qere as canonical, the qere impart amplification to text structure, and Chronicles amplifies Samuel/Kings. In reading such qere in lieu of ketiv, Israel would eventually accept their authority and begin placing them in texts, partly explaining why 2nd-1st century B.C. standard temple manuscripts reflected two text types that differed somewhat.[**] A source of more extensive amplification would provide a main text-type differentiation (see Top. B & C).

It's said the text was consonantal (limited to consonants) until Masoretes invented pointing (vowels) in the Middle Ages. But inspiration took the form of Spirit dictation utilizing writer intell-

* M. Graves, *The Origin of Ketiv-Qere Readings*, Heb. U. Col. Jew. Inst. Rel.
**S. Talmon. 1975. *Qumran and the History of the Biblical Text.* Ed. F.M. Cross & S. Talmon. Harvard U. Press. Cambridge MA. p27

ect,[*] necessitating vowels at text inception for comprehension.[**] Consonantal texts appear in text history, likely due to variant spelling/pronunciation threatening scripture preservation. Use of consonantal texts would hinder this, and written/oral tradition and use of a few consonants as vowels would diminish the threat to help prevent confusion by enabling correct reading, and pointing of the Masoretes would standardize language to end the threat. Such text history would be unadvertised to avoid controversy.

Qere Support, Adapt, Clarify or Advance Ketiv Content

Masorete qere: Clarify or adapt ketiv or offer valid alternatives
Variant grammar: A Jer.8:7 Hebrew word with a ketiv letter *waw* means *horse*, but with a qere *yod* it's *bird*, and *bird* fits the context. Ketiv/qere variance in the letters is common, and qere seem to correct ketiv, but really up-date (adapt) spelling. These letters, originally consonants, later served as vowels too, and the qere would eventually finalize the changing spelling convention.

Qere clarify Hebrew-text gender discord. A ketiv masculine noun (tree), in 1 Kg.19:4, has a feminine adjective (num.1), suggesting the noun was once feminine, or current use of feminine numerals 3-10 with masculine nouns once included 1,2. The qere assigns a masculine numeral, up-dating grammar convention.

Qere vowels are applied to ketiv with no note if the intent is well known. At times a ketiv *he* has unique pointing signifying *she*. Some see this as erratic copying, but it's up-dating of a word earlier noting both genders, as prior-gender masculine language is inclusive of feminine personae (e.g. our *man* includes women). Retaining an early gender-distinction lack and a later distinction allows readers to verify changing spelling convention.

At 1 Kg.15:18 and 2 Kg.15:25, in what's called construct-chain grammar, pointing identifying a definite article is present,

---

* L. Bednar. *The KJB in Relation to Inspiration, Inerrancy and Providential Guidance*. IFBC/WCBS booklet.
** T. Strouse, *Scholarly Myths Perpetuated in Rejecting the Masoretic Text of the Old Testament*. Dean Burgon Society web site.

but a usual definite-article consonant is absent, so this chain was once made definite in abbreviated fashion. Changing grammar convention is indicated, an old convention contrasting with the new at 1 Kg.16:18 and 2 Kg.11:19 where the consonant appears in this chain. The mixed grammar verifies changing convention.

At times variant spelling convention for a term causes varied passage sense, and the qere clarifies this. In 2 Kgs.8:10, Elisha lets a Syrian king think he will survive a disease, but knows he won't survive, a logical rendering indicated by qere spelling. A ketiv-term spelling indicates Elisha either says the king won't survive, missing passage sense, or he asks why would the king not survive, which fits the sense. The qere clarifies the sense.

A valid alternative: Translations may favor ketiv over qere, the ketiv being for all people and the qere for old Israel. The KJB Ps. 100:3 follows the ketiv, saying...*the Lord he is God: it is he that hath made us, and not we ourselves; we are his people, and the sheep of his pasture.* Creation subjects us to God, but many ignore God as if they were the Creator. Like most versions, the NIV renders the qere, saying, *the Lord is God. It is he who made us, and we are his; we are his people, the sheep of his pasture.* The qere advances ketiv emphasis that we belong to God by creation and are obliged to follow Him. But the qere, *and we are his,* isn't needed, for the ketiv is emphatic (*we are his people and the sheep of his pasture*). The matter is one of degree of emphasis. Likely, extra qere emphasis reminded Israel to follow God in days when they often went astray, before the Spirit was permanently endowed. The qere is a valid alternative for all who ignore God.

Canonical minor qere: Ketiv inerrancy advanced/clarified.
In the 2 Kgs.16:6 ketiv, Syrians raid Elath. The qere calls them Edomites (Elath is in Edom), and Isa.7:1 calls them Syrians. Isa. 9:12 notes another raid by Syrians and Philistines, and 2 Chron. 28:17,18 calls them Edomites and Philistines. Ethnic Edomites prove to be Syrians in another sense, vassals of Syria by military defeat. Verifying this, 2 Sam.8:13,14 says David defeats Syrians

in the Valley of Salt in Edom, and 1 Chron.18:12 calls them Edomites. Thus a 2 Kg.16:6 qere amplifies the ketiv, Chronicles clarifies Isaiah and Samuel/Kings, and the qere is canonical. 1 Chronicles is an amplified book, so its verse 18:12 amplifies 2 Sam.8:13 without qere, showing David's victory in the Valley of Salt is figurative, his general Abishai being the literal victor.

The 1 Kg.22:48 ketiv says Jehoshaphat had 10 ships for trips to Tharshish, and the qere says he built them, advancing the ketiv. The 2 Chron.20:36,37 ketiv utilizes the qere, so 2 Chronicles too advances the 1 Kings ketiv and affirms a canonical qere.

A Judges 18:30 qere-like device notes a man's figurative identity in lieu of the literal. The ketiv notes a literal grandson of Moses, but the man's idolatrous nature calls for the figurative, Grandson of Manasseh, an idolator king. This is like calling him a son of the ungodly, Belial. The qere-like reading is canonical, advancing the canonical ketiv in stressing the man's true nature.

A valid alternative: In 2 Sam.16 Hushai offers to be Absolom's counselor, secretly serving David against Absolom, and the ketiv and qere portray a two-sided offer, both applying to the text. In 16:18 a ketiv *not* (same *not* again) makes Hushai's statement read like, I'll not be the chosen king, but I'll abide with him, which seems to challenge Absolom's rule, so it's not in the oral offer. It's an aside questioning who is king, and is literal truth for translations of non-Hebrews, in accord with context revealing Hushai's goal. A qere *his* clarifies the oral offer as Hushai says to Absolom, *whom the Lord and this people…choose, his (or to him) will I be and with him will I abide* (the ketiv requires *but* & the qere *and*). The qere refers only subtly to David, the real choice of God and the people. Subtlety in the oral offer enables non-Hebrews to see the ketiv as an aside, so the qere is canonical, anticipating future Christians and other non-Hebrew readers. The subtlety continues in 16:19, Hushai saying, *whom should I serve…should I not serve in the presence of his son? as I have served in thy father's presence, so will I be in thy presence …*(as he served David in the past, he will now in Absolom's presence).

Canonical major qere: Ketiv inerrancy advanced, God's hand revealed by providential guidance in matters known only to Him.

Progressive revelation by qere: A Job 13:15 qere teaches what men can't know, progressive revelation. It stresses a God-to-man relationship and consequences for failure in this. In the KJB qere-related reading, Job says of God, *Though he slay me, yet will I trust in him: but I will maintain mine own ways* (right conduct) *before him.* The ketiv expresses Job's cry that his righteousness brings adversity, a typical human reaction. [RSV, *Behold, he will slay me; I have no* (same *not*) *hope; yet I will defend my ways to his face*, dishonors God, distorting the ketiv by the later *no/not* sense violating context]. The ketiv human reaction is contrary to God and is to be overcome. A contrasting reaction by the qere stresses righteousness and is expected of God's people at maturity, with permanent Spirit endowment to resist error. It becomes the proper one for Israel in oral readings to foster maturity (Job struggles for maturity in his plight as one who knows he's redeemed- Job 19:25). Oral readings prefigure qere, that in turn prefigure true church versions. The qere amplifies the ketiv, superseding it, as the spirit of the law supersedes the letter, and the KJv example is followed by many. Ketiv status is like that of the letter of the law in ancient Israel when error ruled before permanent Spirit bestowal, revealing the error of God's people from the start. It still applies the way the letter of the law does, to define that which displeases God, and for contrast with the superseding church-era spirit of the law (the law *our schoolmaster to bring us unto Christ*).

Dispensational prophecy by qere: Qere can offer dispensational prophecy, a matter known only to God. A dispensational prophetic Isa.10:32 qere amplifies the ketiv by subtlety as Assyria threatens Jerusalem before Babylonian captivity. The KJB says, *As yet shall he remain at Nob that day: he shall shake his hand against the mount of the daughter of Zion, the hill of Jerus-*

alem. The difference is the qere *daughter* that is *house* in the ketiv, both relating to the Jerusalem-temple hill. The two are equivalent, so the qere seems minor, a ketiv alternative. But *daughter* subtly advances the sense of *house*, the latter relating to historic Israel, all who followed God and all who didn't. *Daughter* introduces dispensational prophecy known only to God, signifying a true future Millennial Israel that will follow Christ (see *daughter of Zion* in Zec.9:9, Jn.12:13-15 & Isa.62:11-12). In Isa.10:24-34 the daughter of Zion is to be secure from hostile nations, and Isa.10: 32 relates to Isa.11 prophecy on Christ in the Millennium gathering Israel from dispersion to subject nations to her. The *house* of Zion was saved from Assyria, but the *daughter* will rule nations. Old Israel of the ketiv contrasts with new Israel of the qere (Zec. 12:10-14). The qere is stressed in oral readings and translations.

Emphasis by qere: Qere advance ketiv by emphasis. In the KJB Isaiah 44:24 qere-related reading, God says...*I am the Lord that maketh all things...that spreadeth abroad the earth by myself* (Heb. *from proximity with me*). For *by myself* the ketiv has, *Who was with me?* God alone is Creator, so ketiv and qere are equivalent. But the ketiv softly asks a question a bit veiled in Hebrew language, and the qere emphasizes the loud answer that so many ignore. The qere is canonical by the divine hand, for God alone has creation knowledge and can answer the ketiv question.

God's Hand on the Text Long after Closing of the Canon

God's name *YHWH*, unlawful for Hebrews to speak, doesn't have vowels. In Exo.3:14 God reveals it to Moses in terms of its meaning, I AM THAT I AM, indicating it's had no vowels since before Pentateuch origination at ~1450 B.C, and likely throughout text history. It's usually rendered the title *LORD*, but in cases where it appears with no other term for God, and a name instead of a title is needed, Masoretes assigned vowels of *Adonai* to yield *Jehovah* that defies linguistics. It isn't the actual pronunciation, and isn't a

Hebrew or Aramaic name, and Hebrew has no *J*. Many deny it's a name of God, but it's long been in the KJB for a good reason. It joins *YHWH*, unutterable name of unapproachable holy God, to *Adonai*, my Lord. This personalizes the name to suggest in the Old Testament, Christ who would later make God personal as our Lord (He taught us to say our *Father* - Mt.6:9). If *YHWH* appears beside *Adonai* in the text, it's given vowels of plural *Elohim* mainly denoting the plurality of God's person, the Trinity. Christ's equality with YHWH in the Trinity is His authority to make God personal.

The link of Christ to *Adonai*, *Elohim* and *Jehovah* indicates that the meaning of YHWH, I AM THAT I AM, revealed by God to Moses in Exo.3:14, links to *Jehovah* as pronunciation of YHWH revealed by God to Moses in Exo.6:3 of the KJB. *Jehovah* looks like an approved name preventing the actual pronunciation. Now Masorete pointing appears in a text that masked knowledge of Christ and the Trinity, and text tradition and KJB translation, practiced long after the canon closed, seem guided by God's hand to prevent actual pronunciation by Gentiles, as well as Hebrews. So why do scholars reject the concept of God's hand on true text copies or a true translation like the KJB to guide His people?

Topic B. Amplification: A Unique Unappreciated Textual Principle

God's hand in text history creates a unique textual aspect, partial revelation of mystery or subtlety in early Old Testament books that's advanced or clarified in later books or the New Testament. Progressive revelation in text composition (amplification) relates to changes for God's people, from creation, to Canaan conquest, to Babylonian exile, to the church, to the Kingdom. Deuteronomy amplifies other Pentateuch books, reiterating with additions on changes in matters like manner of future warfare in Canaan, an established worship place, relations of Levites to priests, of people to prophets & future kings and of people to civil justice. Effects on Deuteronomy content are minor, but are major in Chronicles dealing with Israel's failure to obey God noted in Samuel/Kings. Regarding Old-Testament amplification we consider Hebrew extant Dead-Sea scrolls dating to the 3rd century B.C, the Septuagint translation dating to the 3rd-2nd centuries B.C, the Samaritan Pentateuch version of the Hebrew, dated usually to the 5th-4th centuries B.C. & Aramaic targumim of the 2nd-1st centuries B.C.

Amplification Contained Within the Old Testament Text

We've discussed minor amplification within the Old Testament, canonical margin notes that clarify or advance the text. Now we discuss major amplification in the books of prophets and writings.

Old Testament amplification gave Israel new knowledge of God's plans, and post-exilic Chronicles amplified His near-future will. Among prophetic books, Haggai, Zechariah, Malachi and Isaiah amplified His future plan for a nation that would reject the Messiah and pass away for many centuries in 135 A.D. Ezekiel, Joel, Isaiah and others amplify knowledge of God's far-future final plan about the Tribulation, Armageddon and Millennium.

The Great Tribulation, Armageddon and the Millennium

Isaiah's testimony: Isaiah speaks of a divine child of Israel with the government on His shoulders as He rules on David's throne (9:6,7), referring to Christ in the Millennium. The Millennium is spoken of in terms of great peace, the wolf lying down with the lamb and the child playing at the hole of the poisonous asp (11:6-9). Israel is re-gathered from dispersion at this time (11:11,12).

Joel's testimony: Joel 3:2,11 speaks of Armageddon, all nations gathering for war. Ezk.39:11 and Joel 3:2,14 both place the battle in a valley. Joel 3:14-16 notes a *day of the Lord*, and in 3:16,17 the Lord is the one who will fight for Israel, so He ordained the conflict and controls it. Joel 1:6 speaks of a plague of locusts with teeth like a lion's (1:6), an appearance like that of horses (2:4) and making noise like that of chariots (2:5). Locusts attacked ancient Israel for its unfaithfulness to God, but this event also depicts multitudes attacking Israel at Armageddon in the future.

Ezekiel's testimony: Ezekiel offers much detail advancing our knowledge of Armageddon in Joel. Before discussing this, we must clarify the interpretation of Ezekiel chapters 38 and 39.

Many say Ezekiel 38,39 apocalyptic language prophesies of Russia attacking Israel just before the Tribulation, or at its midpoint. This is based on <u>supposed</u> KJB mistranslation in Ezk.38:2, 39:1. Supposedly Gog, the KJB *chief* (Heb. *rosh) prince*, is a prince of Russia (*rosh* supposedly signifies *Rus*) attacking Israel, and Magog, Meshech and Tubal are allied with Russia.

Rosh is rendered *chief* or an equivalent over 400 times, and is transliterated just once (a man's name, Gen.46:21). If Ezekiel refers to nations, it uses names recognizable as such, not a term signifying a title or a man's name, so *rosh* isn't Russia. And in the Hebrew a pause (disjunctive accent) at *prince* separates it from *rosh*, so *rosh* ties to *Meshech*, and we read *the prince* (pause), *chief of Meshech* [1] (same as KJB *chief prince of Meshech*). *The prince, Rosh of Meshech* is grammatically possible, but *rosh* transliterated will signify a man's name since a common noun will be translated. A suggested, *prince of Rosh, Meshech* is poor grammar/translation (pause misplaced).[*] *Rus* originated long after Ezekiel was written, and *rosh* has no linguistic tie to *Russia.*[2,3,4,5,6,7]

For satanic Russian armies to attack Israel before or during the Tribulation is illogical. Antichrist builds a power base there just before the Tribulation and is in power at the midpoint as Israel is defended by him by his covenant, so the attack would be against him. Magog/Meshech/Tubal signify antichrist allies, not foes. Gog signifies an antichrist figure of north parts (Ezk.38:3,15 – prefigured by ancient Antiochus Epiphanes of Syria, a nation north of Israel), and Magog signifies his nations coalition. Gog's

*A first disjunctive at *prince* has priority over a second that some misapply. Kohlenberger renders the construct, *prince of, chief of, Meshech*...contextually accords with the KJB, but unnecessarily adds the second disjunctive to the first (Kohlenberger, J.R. 1987. *The Interlinear NIV*. Zondervan). Green has *the prince, Rosh of Meshech,* possible grammatically, but poor translation, as noted above (Green, J.P., Sr. 1985. *The Interlinear Bible*. Hendrickson).

Magog is a coalition from all 4 world quarters in Satan's post-Millennial final rebellion (Rev.20:8). The Ezekiel coalition is from the north (39:2) but originates in all 4 world quarters, so Magog is a world coalition, not one from Russian territory. Meshech, Tubal and Gomer are an early part of Magog (Gen.10:2), and nations joining in (Ezk.38:5,6) are Togarmah in the north, Ethiopia in the south, Persia in the east and Libya in the west. The 7 nations, the number of completion in scripture, along with the 4 compass directions, signifies a world coalition.[8] Persia, Ethiopia and Libya were allies of antichrist forerunner Antiochus,[9] so his partial coalition prefigured that of allies of the final antichrist. God is the one who draws the armies, and Russia wouldn't attack antichrist and attempt to defeat its own cause.

Further refuting the notion that the attack on Israel is just before the Tribulation, God's destruction of those armies isn't a prelude to the Tribulation, when antichrist seeks to rise to power, but a conclusion of judgment of Israel's enemies. Ezekiel 39:22 says Israel knows her God from the time of the attack and ever after, so the attack can't shortly precede the Tribulation, a time when Israel is deceived by antichrist.

At times scripture uses *north* in a figurative sense to mean heaven, while *south* means earth (Ps.89:12,13). Christ is from *the north*, heaven (Is.41:25). Lucifer seeks to ascend to *the sides of the north* or heaven (Is.14:12-15). *Evil from the north* (Jer.4:6), refers to Babylon's war with Israel ordained by heaven, for Babylon is east, not north, of Israel. Antichrist figures are of the *north* in the sense that heaven ordains them to punish those of the *south* (earth) that merit God's punishment.

The battle scene: Ezk.38,39 war is that of antichrist on Christ and Israel at Armageddon at the Tribulation climax when a world coalition attacks Israel (Rev.16:14). In Ezk.39:22 all Israel after the war knows the true God *from that day and forward*, which isn't so until after Armageddon. Antichrist's demise on Israel's mountains in Ezk.39:4 is that at Armageddon in Dan.11:45. Ezk.

15

38:21 invaders turn their swords on each other, as in Zec.14:13 at Armageddon. The earthquake, hail and fire of Ezk.38:19,20 are at Armageddon (Rev.11:19,16:18-21). The 1/6 of invaders God spares (Ezk.39:2) are those not drawn to Israel, and those drawn are part of the 1/3 of men killed at Armageddon (Rev.9:18), requiring 7 months to bury (Ezk.39:12). The latter are a feast for birds (Ezk.39:17-20), as at Armageddon (Rev.19:17,18). The rest of the 1/3 die by God's fire on Magog homelands (Ezk.39: 6).

And Ezk.38:11 speaks of Israel at peace, without protective walls, bars and gates, which is not a Tribulation first-half peace of antichrist that scholars suggest. Antichrist wages war as he rises to power in the Tribulation first half, as seen in wars, death and famine of the first 3 judgment seals of Rev.6:1-6 and as forecast by Daniel 11:21-28. Israel will be in conflict at this time and needing protection by walls, bars and gates, real or symbolic. The Ezekiel peace is one God ordains (Ezk.38:14) by millennial covenant (Ezk.37:26), that of the Millennium. Ezekiel includes the Millennium as the main topic of chapters 34-48 (e.g. David rules re-gathered Israel as a nation in Ezk.37:22-24, and nations revere Israel's God in Ezk.39:7, clearly millennial events).

Ezekiel includes in the great battle, Armageddon and satan's final rebellion at the end of the Millennium, in a panoramic day of the Lord. Babylonian war and Israel's captivity and return, major subjects of Ezk.12-24, are a prelude to Armageddon victory that, in turn, is a prelude to the war of the final rebellion that ends all war. In Ezk.38:11,12 armies attack Israel in final rebellion to take spoil from a nation having great riches and peace, that, for Israel, can only be God's Millennial blessing. Ezk.39:2 shows why antichrist and his armies attack at Armageddon, being drawn for judgment (using satan and his agents - Rev.16:14).

Gog/Magog signify an anti-Israel coalition at Armageddon and post-Millennial final rebellion. Gog/Magog disaster (Ezk.38, 39) signifies death to 1/3 of mankind at Armageddon and Satan's army at final rebellion (Rev.20:8,9). Gog's armies disturbing the Millennium die by fire and the Ezk.38:22 heavenly fire relates to that of Rev.20:9 final rebellion, and Ezk.38:22 pestilence relates to Zec.14:12 plague at Armageddon. Ezekiel's reference to both battles is also seen as armies die by fire and sword (Ezk.38:21), the sword being the Word of Christ's mouth at Armageddon (Rev.19:21) destroying by weapons, natural disaster, etc.[*]

Ezk.38,39 judgment by war depicts the defeat of enemies of Israel, past and future. Babylonian war depicts future Armageddon and final rebellion on the far horizon. And Egypt's judgment in Israel's exodus is alluded to, for added to the judgment sword, rain and pestilence is the hail and fire that befell Egypt.

Other prophets join aspects of Armageddon and final rebellion. Jer.25:15-33 depicts Armageddon as nations die by sword (25:31), but heaven's fire of final rebellion is there. Wrath of God in heaven (Jer.25:30), as Christ is on earth (Rev.20:9), signifies fire, for God is a consuming fire in judgment (Heb.12:29). Jer.25 by-passes Armageddon burial of the dead, and lack of burial puts the focus on final rebellion, fire consuming the dead, or earth being burned up (2 Pet.3:10). Zephaniah and Joel allude to a near-future Babylonian war and foretell the far-future Tribulation and Armageddon. But Zeph.3:14-20 also depicts the Millennium, and Zeph.1:2, 3:8 depict destruction and fire of God's jealousy consuming earth and nations, as in final rebellion. In Joel 3:17-21 the city of Jerusalem is free of strangers, which is realized only after the Millennium (Zec.14:16-19) when only saved ones live.

The Old Testament amplified in the New
Further comment on Armageddon: Aspects of Joel prophecy above are further amplified by the New Testament in Revelation. Joel's literal locust attack of Israel is advanced in Rev.9 where

---

*Ezekiel refers to ancient warfare (horsemen, bows, etc.) in Old Testament figurative language suited to the ancients, but symbolizing modern warfare for readers today. Ezk.39:9,10 on wooden enemy weapons used as fuel in place of regular wood sources, is a figurative way of saying that devices used against Israel will be used to supply her needs. Indeed this very thought is noted in Ezk.39:10 as spoilers become the ones spoiled, or robbers the ones robbed.

it's revealed as figurative of multitudes of antichrist's forces set to attack Israel. Imagery of wings with sounds of horse-chariots and teeth of lions, reflects description of the locusts in Joel. A Rev.9 5th trumpet announces release of locusts driven by devils of the bottomless pit, agents of apollyon (satan) moving antichrist forces sent by satan to attack Israel, but turned by God to torment these forces. A 6th trumpet releases 4 mighty angels that destroy antichrist's forces through fiery horsemen that kill a number amounting to 1/3 of all men on earth. Joel's locust attack of Israel is amplified as Israel's deliverance at Armageddon is aided by God's reversal of the locust-type role.

Joel 2:2 calls the *day of the Lord* a day of darkness. In Joel 3:15 the sun, moon and stars are darkened, and Joel 2:31 speaks of the sun turned into darkness and the moon into blood. This corresponds to the same events in the opening of the 6th seal of Revelation 6:12 during the Tribulation. Timing of these events in Revelation amplifies Joel by clarifying the time frame of the Tribulation as one that immediately precedes Armageddon.

More about the Millennium
Israel failed God badly throughout its history as a nation. The priests proved problematic throughout the nation's history, from Aaron, the first priest, who gave idolatrous people a golden calf to worship (Exo.32), to Aaron's sons Nadab and Abihu who offered strange fire on God's altar (Lev.10), to dishonest priests in late pre-exilic days of Jeremiah (Jer.13), to mass idolatry of priests and Levites on the return from Babylon in Ezra's time (Ezra 9). Kings were disobedient to God, from Saul the first king, to Solomon and his later idolatry (1 Kgs.11), to Manasseh's unprecedented idolatry and cruelty in Judah (2 Kgs.21), to the idolatry and lawlessness of the final pre-exilic kings of Judah (2 Kgs.23-25). Solomon's great temple was ruined in Babylonian war on Jerusalem, war that resulted in the Captivity (2 Kgs.25).

Theocracy, the goal: Israel failed at theocracy, but God can't fail. He will make her great in obedience and glory one day, in

18

millennial theocracy by Messiah's rule. Knowledge of theocracy in Isaiah is advanced by Zec.14 and Ezk.40-48 notes on the Old-Testament priesthood and temple in their Millennial form.

Zechariah's testimony: Elements of Judaism will be restored in the Millennium for a restored Israel (Zec.14), but Old Testament institutions were superseded by New Testament ones, so how are old practices like feasts and temple worship restored? Especially difficult to imagine is a restoration of animal sacrifice, for Christ is the superior superseding sacrifice. Such things are restored literally in the kingdom, for they once were God's ordained way for His people, and will be associated with Old Testament saints at that time. But, while the literal institutions themselves will be restored, the literality of their forms must be changed somehow.

Fully literal forms ended in the church era, the letter of the law ending in emphasis on the spirit of the law. Literal forms of Judaism's institutions aren't for the church era, as scripture tells us in speaking of Paul's efforts against Judaizing, the practice of literal elements of Judaism in Christianity. In Gal.2:11-21, Paul scolds Peter for Judaizing in respecting Jewish elitism on eating with Gentiles. In Gal.3 he speaks of the foolishness of seeking justification by the law. In Gal.4:9-11 he scolds Christians for observing elements of the letter of the law like special days. In Rom.2:28,29 he notes literal circumcision replaced by a spiritual type. When in Acts 18:21 Paul says, *I must by all means keep this feast* (Pentecost) *that cometh in Jerusalem,* he isn't observing the law but is attending a feast where he is to fulfill God's will for service, as he reveals in Acts 20:16. Paul was guilty of Judaizing in making an Old Testament sacrifice for purification in the Jerusalem temple in Acts 21, but that was the result of urging by James and the Jerusalem church whose authority he obeyed, and he suffered much for this error.

Fully literal institutions can't be restored in the church era or the kingdom era, especially animal sacrifice to atone for sin. Heb. 10:14 says, *for by <u>one</u> offering he hath <u>perfected forever</u> them* *that are sanctified.* Heb.10:18, speaking of remission in the New Testament era, says, *Now where remission of these is, there is no more offering for sin.* Animal sacrifice was an offering for sin, and Christ ultimately saves Old Testament saints from penalty of sin. The old sacrifice prefigured Christ and can't be restored even for symbolic sin atonement. That would reverse God's plan and dishonor Christ, king of the Millennium. No animal sacrifice for real or symbolic sin atonement in the Millennium is possible. Indeed Israel as part of the church in the Millennium can't be so disparate from others as to practice animal sacrifice, casting doubt on full literality of other Old Testament institutions in that era.

There is a literal aspect to Zec.14, but its extent in an apocalyptic book can vary, and figurative language (not spiritualizing that eliminates literality) is expected. Elements of Judaism noted here, especially animal sacrifice, likely signify the corresponding figurative superseding institutions to be literally observed in the Millennium. It would be necessary to use Old Testament terms in a figurative sense in referring to superseding institutions in a book written over 400 years before Christ's First Advent.

The extent of figurative language would be that to which literalism is not appropriate. Zec.14 indicates Old Testament institutions will be restored in the Millennium, but Hebrews 10: 1-23 tells us the restoration is figurative to a degree. This is indicated by the reference to just one feast in Zec.14, the feast of Tabernacles, a forerunner of the Millennium. The feast finalized the year in Israel as a time to rejoice over harvest ingathering and restoration of the food of life. This corresponds to a superseding fulfillment in the Millennium, the joy of a final ingathering of souls as Christ rules the world and restores spiritual life to Israel. And the feast was preceded by a Day of Atonement to restore Israel from the tragedy of sin that the feast might be joyful. This relates to the Millennium that will be preceded by a national day of mourning to restore Israel from the sin of rejecting Messiah (Zec.12:10-14) and give her kingdom joy. This feast that's to be observed at Israel's millennial restoration, was observed by Judah in beginning national restoration after Babylonian captivity (Ezra 3:4). Thus the feast relates to restoration, the great millennial theme, and Zechariah notes a literal superseding feast much like the old one, but of figurative form suited to the Millennium.

Zec.14:18 notes Egypt punished by lack of rainfall if it does not observe the feast. Egypt symbolizes the world and all Gentile nations in scripture, so this adds to the symbolism sense. Zec.14: 16 speaks of all nations, and 14:18 speaks of Egypt, suggesting interchangeability since no other nation is noted in the verse. Zec.14:19 speaks of Egypt and all nations together, which can be a way to equivalence the two in an all-nations symbolism. *Egypt* is likely a symbolic name here, for the literal Egypt would not suffer much from no rain for failing to come to the feast. Egypt is a nation not dependent on its own rainfall for crop growth, the annual Nile flooding nurturing all significant agriculture.

Zec.14:21 tells of pots for seething sacrifices, with no mention of blood or killing of animals that would indicate actual practice of sacrifice. The verse should refer in some way to sacrifices of passionate praise and good works inherent to New Testament believer-priests (Heb.13:15,16). Pots will signify human vessels in which spiritual sacrifices occur. This correlates with the Zec. 14:21 note on the pots as holy since, from the formal beginning of the church, believers have had the Holy Spirit permanently.

Regarding a Zec.14:20,21 temple suggested by *altar* and *house of the Lord*, this too seems to be Old Testament language symbolic of superseding millennial forms. A literal Tribulation temple is noted in 2 Thess.2:7-12 and Rev.11:1,2, but that temple will be defiled by antichrist, and will likely be destroyed before Christ's millennial rule. The temple can be cleansed (Dan.8:14), but Christ showed He supersedes the literal temple in speaking of His body as a temple as He stood by the literal temple (Jn.2:18-22). Thus continuance of a literal temple in His kingdom isn't likely. A temple building was a temporal place for recognition of

God's place in the lives of His people until the believer's body became God's permanent temple. Antichrist's defiling of the Tribulation temple should signify the end of the literal institution form (and likely aspects of other institutions too). Indeed Rev. 21:22 tells of superseding of the literal temple by Christ and the Father as they rule in the eternal state, the second part of the earthly kingdom, so we expect no literal temple in the first part when Christ rules as God's temple for His people. The millennial temple signifies God's dwelling place with man in the Millennium, as in Ezk.37:26-28. Here God's sanctuary, or tabernacle, is now evermore with his people (includes the eternal state that scripture says has no literal temple). Acts 15:16 (from Amos 9:11) on restoring David's tabernacle would refer to restoring the place of worship for David and Israel in the millennial sense.

Ezekiel's testimony: Ezk.40-48 tells of restored Old-Testament institutions in the kingdom, describing a temple, the old priesthood and literal animal sacrifice with literal blood (Ezk.43:19-25), in reference to the Millennium. The literal animal sacrifice is undeniable, so this refers to a literal Old-Testament kingdom. Fully literal institution forms appear, but application of literality is unique in this largely apocalyptic book, and some language is highly indicative of symbolism and non-literal institution forms.

This is a complex reference to two kingdoms. A potential earthly kingdom existed for Israel at Christ's First Advent, one with literal Old Testament institutions. Christ's sacrifice was predestinated (God's will), but if it hadn't happened, He would have been the ruler of an Old Testament kingdom (man's perspective). Israel potentially could realize this kingdom but forfeited it by disobedience in refusing her Messiah. Thus that kingdom is to be replaced by a millennial one having elements of old institutions noted in Zec.14, but these will be in superseding millennial form just symbolic of what might have been. Ezk.40-48 denotes two kingdoms, one that might have been, with literal institutions, and one that will be, with superseding symbolic ones.

The old kingdom in Ezekiel belonged to Israel, but the nation forfeited it in rejecting the king, necessitating a new one. We're told of a kingdom that might have been (Ezk.43:7), and in telling of its glories, scripture speaks of a better eternal one, notably in Ezk.43:9,44:2,3,9. Scripture unmistakably reveals the eternal one by literal and figurative language in Ezekiel 47, as we'll see.

Now temple property measurements on Israel's behalf signify her ownership, as Rev.11:1,2 tells us, saying the temple outer court isn't measured, for it's given to Gentiles for a time. In Ezk. 40:5-43:17 measurements of the Old-Testament kingdom of Israel with its temple are noted, but Israel's literal future Tribulation temple will be defiled by antichrist (2 Th.2:4) and will likely be removed. Thus in Rev.21:15-23, New Jerusalem, with its temple, is measured, and so belongs to God's people, but in this city of the eternal state, the old temple has been replaced by God the Father and Christ as the new temple for all His people.

If Israel had received Christ, animal sacrifice would likely have continued for redemption. But the fact that Christ superseded those sacrifices further foretells failure of the kingdom that might have been. God made a real kingdom offer to Israel, but foreknew the rejection and the necessary sacrifice of His only begotten Son. He reminds Israel she could have avoided the Tribulation through obedience to the kingdom order presented by Ezra and Nehemiah after the Babylonian Captivity, but ultimately by Christ after His ministry to her at the first Advent.

Strong literal language on the kingdom that might have been is in Ezk.40:2 that refers to a *very high mountain* in Israel as the locale of an immense temple area in Ezekiel 45:1. The size of the temple area is very impractical for a literal mountain location and requires supernatural landscape alteration that could have been accomplished if Israel had received her Messiah. But figurative language is incorporated, for a very high mountain doesn't exist in the territory of Israel, the highest being less than 10,000 feet above sea level. Physical terrain elevation in the Millennium is possible, but there's an allusion here to figurative millennial-era language, for Zec.14:9-31 language is indicative of a future political elevation of Jerusalem. The suggestion is an exalted mountain-like throne of Christ and political exaltation of the city among surrounding lands, the major Zec.14 theme.

Ezk.43:1-7 says God would have dwelled in Israel's temple forever if she had received Messiah. Now language about God dwelling with Israel forever is very positive, so His dwelling in a new temple of the Millennium and eternal state is referenced. The prince of the temple in chapters 44-46 seems to be a high priest above all priests, suggesting Christ as the chief personage in Israel's kingdom that might have been. This is indicated in 44:1-3 where an entrance to the temple area is said to be off-limits to all men, for God entered that way. But *the prince* is to enter and leave that way, indicating He is divine. The prince leads the nation in sacrifice to the Father, as expected of Christ if Israel's priestly kingdom had been realized (He led Israel to the church this way by the Cross, though Israel mostly rejected this). The prince is assigned a humanity, being said to have sons to whom He gives an inheritance (Ezk.46:17,18). This signifies Christ as potential ruler of the old kingdom where He would have spiritual sons by salvation, to whom He gives a kingdom inheritance. This too foretells failure of Israel's old kingdom and institutions, and superseding of them by the millennial kingdom and its institutions.

Figurative Ezk.47:1-12 language, relating to a temple and a very high mountain as the temple locale, is striking. The passage notes water issuing out under the threshold of a house in the Millennial-temple area, creating a stream that deepens with distance from the house until it becomes a river. The waters heal living things they contact, except miry marshy places (stagnant water) that are saline (salted). The passage tells of river banks with trees that give eternal fruit new in various months and have never-fading leaves that are for healing. Also noted are fishermen who use nets to catch fish of every kind in the river.

Such language is highly figurative. A literal stream of water doesn't issue out of a building (Ezk.47:1,2) and does not steadily deepen as it flows down a high mountain, growing from a small shallow stream to a great river (47:3-5). It's unlikely God would repeal laws of nature He instituted and called good at creation.

Ezekiel language advanced by Revelation: This apocalyptic language is suggestive of Revelation 22 where the river of water of life from the throne of God's sanctuary (not literal water, for water signifies life) nourishes trees on its banks. The trees give fruit each month and have leaves for healing of the nations. This language is highly figurative, so that of Ezekiel would be too. The Revelation river of life advances details on the Ezekiel river.

God's voice of *many waters* (Rev.14:2, Ezk.43:2) is a river, an uninterrupted flow of His Word of blessing that deepens as it flows further out from His immense <u>mountain-like sanctuary and throne</u> (Water of life by God's salvation Word – Rev.22:17). In Rev.22 the river is in the eternal-state kingdom, but Ezekiel tells us it flows in the millennial era also, as expected, for blessings by God's Word should be multiplied in the Millennium. An ever-deepening river of His far-reaching Word signifies growing blessing that has flowed throughout world history and will flow in the Millennium, bringing blessing to more and more people. Water of life from God's throne will flow as Christ rules the world visibly, by His Word. Living water also signifies people (Rev.17:15), who are "containers" of life, so the ever-deepening river of life also signifies souls added to the river of life in Christ as the Word reaches out to the earth. Marshy miry lands of saline stagnant water left unhealed by the river signify souls who don't join the stream of blessing, not responding to the gospel. This includes those who join satan in the final rebellion against Christ after the Millennium. In Revelation 22, the day of salvation ends, and the river is for God's redeemed people alone.

Trees nourished by the river signify people established in faith by God's Word, as noted in Ps.1:3 that prefigures elements of Ezekiel's prophecy. Here the man established in God's law, or Word, is, *like a tree planted by the rivers of water, that bringeth forth his fruit in his season: his leaf shall not wither*. The non-withering leaf signifies undiminished life in established saints produced by God's Spirit, continuing to bring the gospel for spiritual healing to the nations throughout history. And fruit-bearing signifies the ongoing godly life of saints that has fed their testimony and produced salvation fruits throughout history.

Established souls were first won to Christ themselves, and the fish and nets signify the church era when many souls come to Christ. Fish and nets are reminiscent of Christ's selection of fishermen to preach the Gospel and His metaphorical likening of winning souls to catching fish. Fish and nets likely also signify the many souls that will come to Christ in the millennial era.

In Ezk.47:8,9 healing waters of Jerusalem bring life to what they contact, and heal an unnamed sea. Water flowing to the sea suggests water of God's Word (Eph.5:26) flowing to people. A *sea* signifies people in Rev.13:1, and *waters* like seas in Rev.17:1,15 signify people. There's allusion to the literal Dead Sea, some in the *sea* being sin-dead souls never receiving life, even with input of millennial-era water of life from God (a reason the millennial-era unsaved merit ultimate white-throne judgment).

This Ezekiel passage links to Zec.14:8 *living waters* flowing from Jerusalem to the *former sea* and *hinder sea*. In Zechariah *former sea* signifies pre-millennial saints in resurrected bodies, and *hinder sea* millennial people in natural bodies, all receiving of God's river of life by His Word. Sinful souls need healing of sin's effects, and sinless souls need energy of life from God for eternality. This figurative interpretation fits these passages in Ezekiel and Zechariah. But the fit vanishes if, as scholars say, Ezekiel waters heal physically, reducing salinity of Zechariah's former sea (the Dead Sea) to promote fish and plant life. That would mean Zechariah's hinder sea (Mediterranean) is to receive healing to support fish and plant life, but this sea has abundant fish and plant life now, not requiring healing.

Ezekiel projects beyond the Millennium unto the eternal state in Ezk.47:1-5 comment on the river of life of Revelation 22. The eternal state clearly appears in comments on gates of the temple city in Ezk.48:31-34 that speaks of the city gates inscribed with names of Israel's 12 tribes, as is also said of the city New Jerusalem of the eternal state in Rev.21:10-13. Thus superseding symbolic aspects of Israel's kingdom that might have been will prevail in the eternal state and the Millennium.

Now some Old Testament passages seem to restore relationships of Israel with hostile neighbors in the Millennium. A case in point is Isaiah 11 where the people groups noted can't be identified today. Well the fact that we can't identity the people doesn't mean God can't. But language in passages like Isaiah 11 necessarily invokes ancient identities so that readers of that era of history could understand the teaching. For generations that are much later in history, the wording is symbolic of enemies that have superseded the old ones, but behave in about the same way toward Israel. One look at modern-day Egypt, Syria, Iran and others reveals ancient hatreds and associations concerning Israel continuing in people with a genetic relationship to the earlier enemies. A spirit of hostile relationships with Israel is intact in these people, so the effect today is much like the ancient one.

Amplification for the New Testament and Select New and Old Testament Translations

Now we begin discussing Old-Testament texts that vary from the Masoretic due to amplification. The main amplification source of the variance would be a Hebrew-Text edition that paralleled the standard text late in pre-New Testament history. The parallel text is seen today in Hebrew Dead Sea scrolls with Septuagint (LXX) character, reflecting the fact that the Septuagint translation (and targumim) had an amplified Hebrew-text basis. Many amplified manuscripts are likely extinct, for God's plan evidently was the obsolescence of texts that could compete with the Masoretic Text.

Amplification, a form of inspiration in the Hebrew basis of the LXX, is largely preserved even in highly corrupt LXX texts like those of Vaticanus and Sinaiticus. But its perfect form would appear in an original LXX and its Hebrew basis, and it appears at times in the New Testament as Christ and His disciples quote the Old Testament. The LXX and its Hebrew-text basis weren't to compete with the Masoretic Text, but would be an interim source of vital Christology for the 1st-century church.

The interim texts explain some New Testament quotes of the Old favoring the LXX over the Masoretic, especially in Christology. Some bible-believers doubt an LXX existed before the church era, thinking oldest extant 4th-century LXX manuscripts just repeat New Testament quotes of the Old. But that doesn't explain why New Testament quotes differ from the Masoretic, casting doubt on New-Testament inerrancy. It doesn't explain 2nd-3rd century LXX-type Greek translations by Jews to combat church use of LXX Christology (the Theodotion, Symmachus & Aquila texts). Agreement of the New Testament and LXX testifies of an authoritative amplified LXX-type Hebrew text, and New and Old Testament inerrancy require this authoritative text, as we'll see.

The LXX and its Hebrew basis were temporal authorities that had to be removed from circulation to prevent competition with the standard text. When the New Testament appeared, an LXX-type text wasn't needed, and removal was needful since churches couldn't maintain two somewhat-different Old Testament texts. Evidently LXX abandonment was enacted by text corruption greatly diminishing reliability. Corruption reached an extreme in Vaticanus and Sinaiticus, two 4th century A.D. LXX manuscripts best left in oblivion, but their late added New-Testament portions were made the main basis of modern-version New Testaments.

Amplification in the Septuagint
Amplification in the LXX, from its amplified Hebrew basis, clarified standard-text Christology, so it was vital to the church

in the 1st century. LXX unveiling of Christology isn't surprising in this crucial work preceding closing of the canon by the New Testament. The church had to know its relationship to Christ in better terms than the standard Hebrew text offered in the pre-church period. An evangelistic missionary church could not, at any time, be without inerrant written guidance on Christology basic to its mission. An LXX Hebrew-text basis with amplification is a compelling deduction. How else do we explain open Christology in a Greek translation made well before the First Advent, ~300 years before in the case of the Pentateuch of <u>Hebrew</u> scholars?

It was no accident that a Greek Old Testament had pervaded the Hellenist Jewish community throughout geographical areas populated by Greek-speaking Christians of most of the church of the 1st-century. This Christological Greek Old Testament met the need of this church until the advent of the permanent Greek New Testament. Common familiarity with the LXX would be a reason why Christ and His disciples quoted the Old Testament at times from the LXX, or its Hebrew basis personally translated.

LXX-type Amplification in New Testament Quotes of the Old
New Testament writers often quoted the Old in a general LXX form, in lieu of the Masoretic Text. No current LXX manuscript fully reflects the New Testament quotes, indicating all LXX texts are corrupted from an original form preserved in the quotes.

Hebrews-epistle amplification: LXX Influence is strong in the Hebrews epistle. The epistle scholarship is praised much,[10,11] but some say the author at times quotes the LXX when it supposedly mistranslates the Hebrew,[12] which is just a case of ignorance. The Old Testament is an inerrant account of God's will given when partial enlightenment and mystery marked the text, and the New Testament is God's inerrant account clarifying such matters, as in its quotes of LXX-type variance from the Hebrew. Its writers providentially adopted LXX-type amplification of veiled New Testament concepts in the Old Testament.

Old Testament partial revelation and mystery amplified in an original LXX and the New Testament: Scholars disdaining Hebrews-epistle quotes of LXX variance from the Hebrew forget the inspired New Testament writer isn't just a translator. Divine guidance directs him to amplification of Old Testament mystery and partial revelation. 2 Peter 2:7 illustrates this, emphasizing Lot's true righteous vexation over Sodom's sin. Genesis does not emphasize this, just noting his discomfort over the city vile life-style and emphasizing his mistakes and misfortune in Sodom.

Enlightenment on the standard Hebrew text appears in LXX-type quotes in the New Testament amplifying the Hebrew. Christ and the disciples quote an LXX-type text, authorizing amplification.[13] They would quote the standard text when amplification isn't involved, explaining their quotes of this type at times. Variance amplifies partial revelation, mystery or subtlety, as seen below.

1. Christ in an original 3rd–2nd Century B.C. LXX

LXX amplifying of partial revelation and mystery is seen at Ps. 40:6. Heb.10:5 reflects the LXX, the speaker, the pre-incarnate Christ, telling of His body as prepared for sacrifice. The Hebrew text differs, the speaker telling of His ears opened to God's will.[14]

a. Psalm 40:6 quoted in Hebrews 10:5,6 of the KJB
...when he cometh into the world, he (Christ) *saith, Sacrifice and offering thou wouldest not, but a body hast thou prepared me. In burnt offerings and sacrifices for sin thou hast had no pleasure.*

b. LXX: Psalm 40:6 translation in modern English
Sacrifice and offering you didn't desire; a body you prepared for me; whole burnt offering and sacrifice for sin You didn't require.

c. Hebrew Masoretic Text: KJB translation of Psalm 40:6
Sacrifice and offering thou didst not desire; mine ears hast thou opened: burnt offering and sin offering hast thou not required.

Messiah's sacrifice is veiled in the Hebrew-text Ps.40:6, only the first step, opening of His ears, being given. This led to sacrifice of His body to fulfill His mission. The LXX and New Testament reveal the fulfillment to the church. The vicarious sacrifice was unknown to Israel that saw Messiah only as a king (2nd Advent status), but would be revealed in the church era when the church needed this. As an authoritative text available before the advent of the permanent New Testament, the amplified Hebrew text, via the original LXX, met the need. The LXX Hebrew text gave, and the New Testament preserved, Christology vital to churches.

2. Jesus' healing ministry: Isa.61:1,2 quoted in Lk.4:18,19.

a. KJB English translation of Isa.61:1,2 in Luke 4:18,19.[*]
The Spirit of the Lord is upon me, because he hath anointed me to preach the gospel to the poor; he hath sent me to heal the broken-hearted, to preach deliverance to the captives, and recovering of sight to the blind, to set at liberty them that are bruised, to preach the acceptable year of the Lord.

b. Current LXX text at Isa.61:1,2 translated in modern English
The Spirit of the Lord is upon me, because he has anointed me; he has sent me to preach glad tidings to the poor, to heal the broken in heart, to proclaim liberty to the captives, and recovery of sight to the blind; to declare the acceptable year of the Lord.

c. Hebrew Masoretic Text: English translation in the KJB
The spirit of the Lord God is upon me; because the Lord hath anointed me to preach good tidings unto the meek; he hath sent me to bind up the broken-hearted, to proclaim liberty to the captives, and the opening of the prison to them that are bound. To proclaim the acceptable year of the Lord...

Luke/LXX *recovering of sight to the blind*, isn't in the Masoretic Text, and the Luke/LXX *to preach/proclaim deliverance/liberty to the captives* restates the Masoretic, *opening of the prison to them that are bound*. Further, Luke/LXX *heal* contrasts with *bind up* in the Masoretic, and Luke/LXX *poor* is *meek* in the Masoretic.

---

[*] LXX verse links to a Hebrew text like that in some Dead-Sea scrolls (Brenton, *The Septuagint LXX: Greek and English*. London. 1851).

Amplification advances the nature of healing by Christ. The Hebrew text notes spiritual healing, but implies the physical by broad terminology. Hebrew-text *bind up the broken hearted* and *opening of the prison to them that are bound* specify the spiritual but imply a physical (*broken-hearted* signifies penalty for sin, implying hurt in physical hardship of sin). *Opening of the prison* has a spiritual sense of freeing people from a dark prison of sin and implies the physical for those in a dark prison of physical blindness). Luke and the LXX advance language to include physical healing common to Jesus' ministry (e.g. *recovery of sight to the blind* and *heal* in both and *bruised* in Luke), indicating physical healing accompanying the spiritual of the Hebrew text. Both types appear at times in Jesus' ministry (Mt.9:1-8), so the LXX emphasizes the ministry as the futuristic one of Jesus with dual benefit. And Luke/LXX *poor* specifies one class of the *meek*, the *poor*, as primary recipients of both types of healing.

3. Jesus our salvation. Isa.40:5 portion quoted at Lk.3:6
a. KJB English translation of Isa.40:5 at Lk.3:6
...and all flesh shall see the salvation of God.

b. Current LXX text at Isa.40:5 translated in English
...and all flesh shall see the salvation of God.

c. Hebrew Masoretic Text: KJB English translation
...and all flesh shall see it together

The Masoretic Text refers to all flesh together preparing for the work of God who will correct the error of men, and the New Testament and the LXX advance this, revealing the nature of this work of God as the salvation by Jesus Christ.

4. In the Name of Jesus: Isa.42:3,4 quoted in Mt.12:20,21

a. KJB English translation of Isa.42:4 in Mt.12:20,21
A bruised reed shall he not break...till he send forth judgment unto <u>victory</u>. And in his name shall the Gentiles <u>trust</u>

b. Current LXX text at Isa.42:3,4 translated in modern English

A bruised reed shall he not break...but he shall bring forth judgment to truth...*and in his name shall the Gentiles* trust.

c. Hebrew Masoretic Text: KJB English translation
A bruised reed shall he not break...he shall bring forth judgment unto truth...*and the isles shall wait for his* law.

Matthew reflects the LXX on trusting Christ. The Masoretic Text speaks of the old sense of the law, yet His meekness implies the new spirit of the law based on trust in Him due to ultimate love expressed by His sacrifice for us. Old truth of the law brought judgment, but His salvation is ultimate truth offering victory in changed judgment. Matthew and the LXX advance Masoretic-Text language from the old sense of law, fulfilling the implied sense of the new spirit of the law. And Matthew advances LXX and Masoretic-Text old judgment truth to new judgment victory.

5. A Little Lower Than Angels or a Little Lower Than God?
The LXX amplifies Hebrew-text terms ambiguous by Hebrew brevity of expression and multiple word sense. Context is crucial and often requires a rendering that isn't the usual. Heb.2:7 reflects the LXX Ps.8:5 in saying God made man a little lower than angels. The Hebrew for *angels* is *elohim*, usually rendered *God*. Targumim and Jewish commentators favor *angels*.[15] The word is plural and can refer to non-divine personages, angels or men of high authority representing God. Christ used it to refer to men of high authority (Jn.10:34-35), so it can't always refer to God. In Ps.97:7 it refers to angelic gods who worship the true God, and the epistle writer rendered the LXX *angels*.

But the NASV has *God*. Now Ps.8:5 refers to present and past men who aren't made (created) a little lower than God. Men are infinitely lower in all respects, but are inferior to created angels in limited degree by knowledge, power and dwelling place. It's logical to speak of a creation order with small differences among created beings. It's nonsensical to suggest earthly man being made just a little lower than the infinite creator of Gen.1.

The New Testament advances amplification in the LXX
Christ the ultimate answer to idol worship: LXX progressive Christological amplification clarifies Dt.32:43 mystery, and the New Testament advances this. Heb.1:6 requires angels to worship Christ at His Incarnation, agreeing with the LXX Dt.32:43 that's longer and more detailed than it is in the Masoretic Text. The latter doesn't note angels, only a call to the nations to rejoice in God's justice and mercy for deliverance from idol worship.

Deut. 32:43 quoted in part in the New Testament in Heb.1:6

a. New Testament: Deuteronomy 32:43 portion in the KJB
And again, when he bringeth in the firstbegotten into the world, he saith, And let all the angels of God worship him.

b. Current LXX text translated in modern English
Rejoice you heavens, with Him, and let all the angels of God worship Him; rejoice you Gentiles, with His people, and let all the sons of God strengthen themselves in Him; for he shall avenge the blood of His sons, and he shall render vengeance, and recompense justice to His enemies, and will reward them that hate Him; and the Lord shall purge the land of His people" (final underlined portion is corrupted).

c. Hebrew Masoretic Text: English translation in the KJB
Rejoice, O ye nations, with his people: for he will avenge the blood of his servants, and will render vengeance to his adversaries, and will be merciful unto his land, and to his people.

In the Hebrew-text Deuteronomy 32, God uses oppressors to chastise Israel for worship of idol gods. The tone is very negative until the conclusion in verse 43 where there's a call to rejoice over God's deliverance. God's mercy to His people is seen, and His justice is seen in the punishment of the oppressors. With the passage general negative tone, the only hint of Christology is an allusion in a final joyful tone on deliverance from false worship that doesn't specify the reason for the joy.

But the LXX Deuteronomy verse introduces a clear Messianic tone with, *Let all the angels of God worship him* in the call to rejoice. It identifies worshipping gods of the Hebrew-text Ps.97:7 as *angels (worship him all ye gods)*,[5] tying Dt.32:43 to the Ps. 97-98 theme. This gives fuller meaning in calling angels to worship Christ, the ultimate reason for the call to nations to rejoice by salvation that delivers from idol worship. Here in Psalms idol-worship error is expounded, but in triumph, righteousness and light prevailing in Ps.98. In the joyful tone of 98:3 it's said all the ends of the earth have seen the salvation of God, indicating the world-wide New Testament answer to idol worship. In similar Acts 13:47 language, salvation in Christ extends from Israel to the ends of the earth. In identifying the role of angels, LXX amplification indicates salvation as the reason for joy.

In the Hebrew text the role of angels isn't visible. And without knowledge of the Psalms association, a Messianic aspect of the Deuteronomy verse, isn't visible to Israel that knew little of Christ. The LXX providentially amplified the veiled message of the Hebrew Deuteronomy verse, showing the reason for joy as salvation by Christ, the answer to idol-worship. Amplification is striking, the positive tone of Psalms 97-98 contrasting with a generally negative Deuteronomy 32 tone. The Hebrews epistle reinforces all this, so the New Testament and the LXX give the church a crucial doctrine not given to Israel, the ultimate New Testament solution to the Deuteronomy idol-worship problem.

The Hebrews epistle writer goes a step further in amplification, defining qualifications of He who is the ultimate solution to the idol-worship problem. He reveals a veiled logic tie of prophetic Ps.97-98 to Ps.2:7-12. Ps.2:7-12 says the Son of God, on the day He was begotten (incarnated), was declared ruler of the heathen (Gentiles) to the uttermost parts of the earth and the object of men's trust (Savior). This clear Messianic passage is tied by logic to Ps.97-98 that elucidates and specifies to the church the office and authority of He who defeats idol worship. The Hebrews epistle writer declares the logic tie of the two Psalms passages in a chronological tie of Ps.97:7 worshipping angels to the Begotten Son of Ps.2:7. He does so in his Heb.1:6 note that angels were to worship the First-Begotten when God brought Him into the world. Thus the writer reveals that the day the angels of Ps.97:7 were told to worship Christ was the day of the Incarnation of Ps. 2:7 (see Lk.2:13,14). All this is further logical since it indicates God told angels at the time of the Incarnation, appropriately, that Christ's bodily form in no way diminished His deity. Thus the Hebrews-epistle writer shows the joyful triumph of true worship over idol worship as the divine Christ is revealed in human form. The writer reveals previously-veiled logical/chronological ties of two Hebrew-text Psalms passages, expanding LXX amplification as part of New Testament completion of God's revelation.

Regarding Jesus as deity in human form, the Hebrews writer addressed the anti-Trinitarianism, prevalent in Gnosticism and Arianism in the early church and in contemporary religion. Such religion would make worship of Christ another form of idolatry, rather than the ultimate solution. Thus connection of passages on idol-worship evils to Messianic passages is no surprise. And the authenticity of LXX and Hebrews-epistle passages that provide edification on such concepts should never be in question, the issue being assured by the authority of the New Testament.

LXX Amplification Applied to Translations of the Hebrew Old Testament in the Church Era

The LXX clarifies Hebrew text mystery for O.T. translations
Hebrew-text partial-revelation passages that Providence made mysterious by word ambiguity, will be clarified in the church era when the Hebrew text is translated. Clarification is needed when essential to explain former mystery, but can be unnecessary, as in the case of the Ps.97:7 passage quoted in Heb.1:6 where the LXX and the Hebrew-text renderings *angels* and *gods* are inter-changeable. Neither word invokes loss of meaning, for the basic

sense is that all creatures of higher power are subject to Christ. The Hebrew text can present *gods* to the church, for all gods, including angels and men of high authority, are subject to Christ always. *Angels* in the LXX and New Testament is consistent with the Hebrew text, for if superior angels are subject to Christ, all men, lesser beings, are understood to be subject also.

The legitimacy of *angels* here shows us the KJB *angels* as the rendering for *Eloihim* in Ps.8:5-6 noted earlier is correct. We can't assume *angels* to be correct here if, as indicated in the NASV, man is only a little lower than God. If that were the case, he'd be superior to angels, and subjection of angels to Christ wouldn't automatically specify that all men are in subjection to Christ. An NASV rendering that allows the notion that some authoritative men might not be subject to Christ is clearly wrong.

A need to clarify the Hebrew text in Old Testament translations to reveal former mystery is another aspect of amplification.

1. A virgin or a young woman shall bear a son? Isa.7:14

Therefore the Lord himself shall give you a sign; Behold, a virgin shall conceive, and bear a son, and shall call his name Immanuel.

The Hebrew for *virgin*, *almah*, often refers to a young woman or a maiden, but can be rendered *virgin*, and context determines word sense. *Young woman* doesn't fit context since a young woman bearing a son is no sign at all, being very common. *Maiden* isn't proper since immorality is associated with an unmarried woman who is with child. But total purity and divine intervention are associated with a virgin that is with child.

Scholars suggesting *young woman* advocate using the definite article with *almah*,[16] saying a birth of a son of a certain unknown young woman would be a sign fulfilling the prophecy, but that's wrong. Countless unidentified young women have sons, and no reader throughout the ages could know which one, and which of her son's births, is the sign of the prophecy fulfillment. The Isaiah passage says God expects the sign to be recognized (i.e. *the Lord himself shall give you a sign*). But the whole world would one day see that only the birth of the first son of Mary qualifies when *almah* is rendered *virgin*.

Context indicates *virgin* as the true sense of *almah* here, for a virgin bearing a son would be an ultimately-unique sign. An ancient Hebrew didn't know the significance of this future event associated with the Messiah. He couldn't interpret the verse, in keeping with the plan for veiled Christology for ancient Israel. Providence unveiled the mystery at the dawn of the church era by the LXX *virgin* of the amplified Hebrew text (*parthenos* in Greek), giving full Messianic significance. The New Testament providentially followed this in quoting the Isaiah passage from the LXX. Thus only at the dawn of the church era is the word ambiguity removed and passage mystery revealed. Only then is it possible to translate the word rightly from Hebrew. At this point the mystery of Christology has been revealed, and reverence in interpreting this passage is needed. Thus it becomes necessary to render *almah* in Isaiah *virgin* in translations for the church. The inerrant Hebrew text is unchanged, and the sense of *almah* veiled in ancient days is clarified. Contrast of the indefinite term with the rendering of translations of the Old (and New) Testament announces completion of the revelation in the church era. And lest any who desire to know of this contrast not understand the ambiguity of *almah*, Providence has allowed railing of scholar-skeptics on the subject to make all interested parties aware of all the facts. Thus a modern rendering of *almah* as *young woman* or *maiden* mistranslates the Hebrew, obscuring the true meaning by violating a context that is now fully understood.

Elsewhere in the Hebrew text, *almah* will refer to a young woman or maiden or another virgin in another context. It's for the reason of variant context that a Hebrew or Greek word can't always be translated in the same way from one verse to another (As already noted, this was also the case with *Elohim* in Psalm 8:5). KJB translators were careful to tell us this in a preface note

38

that a given word doesn't have the same sense everywhere.[17]

LXX amplification clarifies the sense of an ambiguous word to reveal prophecy fulfillment of Messianic importance.

2. They pierced my hands and feet, or like a lion my hands and feet? Psalm 22:16 amplifies Hebrew-text partial revelation clarified in church-era translations. The verse in amplified form isn't preserved in the New Testament, but in the LXX-type Old Testament translations of eastern and western churches. When the Masoretic Text reappeared in 16th-century Reformation days, the true church didn't lose this amplified verse. God does not fail His church, for the KJB, like true ancient versions of history, follows the LXX here instead of the normal Hebrew, likely due to recognition that the LXX clarified a Hebrew-text Messianic mystery. The amplified verse must have been preserved in a 17th-century LXX text, as well as ancient versions. God preserved His revelation, guiding KJB translators to reveal His authorization of them to translate His Word. Later translators followed suit, seeing the wisdom of this course, but they often select LXX renderings due to mere intellectual preference.

Comparing the LXX and Masoretic texts reveals veiled prophecy fulfilled by providential amplification. The Masoretic has, *like a lion my hands and my feet*, and the LXX amplifies the verse to reveal it as Messianic, rendering, *they pierced my hands and my feet*. Historically, the Jews were said to alter the passage in the Masoretic to remove the reference to Christ, and Christians were accused of adding it in the LXX. All this is most unlikely given the reverence of both camps for scripture. Actually Providence ordained a change, amplifying Messianic revelation to clarify it. What the Masoretic Text says in veiled fashion, by partial wording and symbolism, is that the fury of the roaring lion Satan was unleashed on someone, in an assault involving the hands and feet (today we would read, *Like a lion* they attacked me, as *they pierced my hands and feet*). The common portion, *my hands and my feet* ties the two texts, and LXX amplification adds the crucial words

39

they pierced. This unveils the meaning in the Masoretic Text and gives us the rest of the language to show the assault as piercing of Christ's hands and feet on the Cross by empowerment of satan symbolized by a roaring lion (KJB 22:13). Amplification advances passage language to present its Messianic importance.

Thus, contrary to scholars, the Masoretic-Text note on a lion is very appropriate. This is the right symbolic reference to the ultimate enemy of Christ in the Crucifixion, as seen by comparing verse 16 with verses 20-21 in the KJB Psalm 22. In this comparison both the KJB and Masoretic Text speak of dogs (Roman soldiers disrespectful of true God and man) around the crucified Messiah. And both the KJB and Masoretic text speak of a deliverance sought from the power of the dog and the lion's mouth. This shows the relevance of the unique Masoretic-Text reference to the lion, in lieu of piercing. What we learn by comparing verse 16 with verses 20-21 in the KJB is that the power of the Roman-soldier dog derives from the mouth of the roaring (lying) lion satan, the accuser of Christ in the person of the lying priests and scribes. The Masoretic-Text unique note on the lion is fully relevant since it reveals the same symbolism of an alliance of dogs and a lion attacking Christ noted in the KJB verses 20,21 and the Masoretic Text. As expected of an unamplified text with a veiled message, the Masoretic Text presents the mysterious lion/dog alliance in both places. In verse 16 the KJB, following the amplified LXX, clarifies the mysterious words, identifying them as the very words in the mind of Jesus on the Cross, words known only to God. The KJB Ps.22:16 words mark the Roman-soldier dogs and lying priests and scribes as empowered by the lying roaring lion satan in a cruel attack in the piercing of Jesus.

In the New Testament era, Masoretic-text mystery is clarified in church translations, for the mystery is past, and prophecy fulfillment is noted. Thus the amplified Hebrew and the original LXX texts served as a bridge that transferred amplified Old-Testament Christology to the New Testament. KJB translators obviously recognized this, but modern translators miss the vital relationship of Masoretic-Text and LXX renderings here, most preferring to imagine a contradiction and making it necessary for us to study to understand the role of amplification here.

3. The role of a divinely-amplified Hebrew text: Now how can the LXX clarify Psalm 22:16 mystery? It draws on the providential Hebrew-text edition of late pre-New-Testament history, a text kindred to the Masoretic and differing only by amplification in part. Amplification of the Masoretic Text, visible in post-exilic books that stem from Ezra (see p56-58), began earlier in a process visible in LXX-type Hebrew Dead-Sea-scroll texts.

Ps.22:16 reveals an amplified text paralleling the standard text in late pre-church times. In most standard manuscripts, the ketiv *Like a lion my hands and my feet* veils Christology, but a few standard manuscripts and qere, a Hebrew Dead-Sea scroll and ancient versions, teach amplification indicative of a parallel amplified Hebrew text, saying, *they pierced my hands and feet.* KJB translators saw the significance, and with ancient Old Latin, Septuagint and Peshitta versions, rightly rendered the verse for the church, *For dogs have compassed me: the assembly of the wicked have inclosed me: they pierced my hands and my feet.* Ps. 22:21 resolves the lion mystery, relating all ketiv and qere by the full meaning. The symbolism and partial language are seen as Christ is openly declared in the church era, and the ketiv lion has a role now evident in Ps.22. The KJB edifies churches, amplifies ketiv mystery and shows that a lion/dog alliance will cause cruel piercing of Jesus. The Ps.22:16 ketiv in amplified texts is dispensational change to edify an Israel that will accept the amplified text and follow Christ in the Millennium (Zec.13:6-9,12:10).

Original LXX-text wording lost in the current texts
Much is corrupt in the current LXX text, as at Leviticus 11 on identities of animals Jehovah said were unclean for His Hebrew people. The NIV reflects corruption regarding animal identities.

Leviticus 11:29,30

NIV: *Of the animals that move about on the ground, these are unclean for you: the weasel, the rat, any kind of great lizard, the gecko, the monitor lizard, the wall lizard, the skink and the chameleon.*

The NIV lists six types of lizards. The translators evidently had no idea of identities of most animals signified by Hebrew terms here, for it's not credible to note all these specific lizard types when other creeping animals would be of concern. Translators today rely on Hebrew-English lexicons, and the lexicon authors admit they're not certain of identities in the six cases. They offer their best guesses, which are poor, as evident when they appear together in one context in Leviticus 11. The problem here is lost knowledge, some ancient Hebrew terms now being obscure.

In a case like this, one must rely on the oldest authoritative source, and the 1611 KJB is the oldest reliable reference among English versions. The KJB Leviticus passage reads as follows:

KJB: *These also shall be unclean unto you among the creeping things that creep upon the earth; the weasel, and the mouse, and the tortoise after his kind, And the ferret, and the chameleon, and the lizard, and the snail and the mole.*

With just two references to lizards, this is far more logical than the NIV. The *lizard* and *chameleon* cover the full spectrum of lizards, the latter being a unique type of lizard. Regarding the source of KJB animal identities, the list is like that in the Brenton LXX text published in 1851 in England, so KJB translators referenced the LXX. But the identities in this LXX text are a bit different from those in the KJB, the KJB *tortoise* and *snail* being called a *lizard*, and a *newt* (a lizard-like amphibian), respectively. The LXX calls the KJB *lizard* an *evet*, a type of lizard, so this isn't a real difference. The order in which animals are listed is the same in the KJB and LXX, so KJB translators consulted the LXX, though the two differences must be explained.

The Brenton LXX over-emphasizes lizards less than the NIV and so is based on a less-corrupt text here. With corruption so common in current LXX texts, a text close to the Brenton, but earlier and uncorrupted, was available to KJB translators. Now if, as this writer proposes, an original LXX translates a text close to the Masoretic, the latter will contain most terms, enabling us to check meanings. To do so we note that one Hebrew name is often given to subjects inherently different, but having figurative or literal resemblance. *Tortoise* is right since the Hebrew for this appears at two other places in the Masoretic Text and is translated by terms confirming this identity. In Num.7:3 the KJB has *covered wagons*, and the similarity to a tortoise is the covering shell and slow motion common to both. And in Isa.66:20 the KJB translates it *litters* in the sense of stretchers bearing the sick or wounded, which is indicative of slow motion, again in common with a tortoise (the Hebrew means, to move gently). The term for *snail* appears nowhere else in the Old Testament, so it can't be checked, but a snail leaves a trail of mucous as it travels and would be considered unclean. KJB translators likely had recourse to an LXX text now lost, but reflecting here an accurate original text relating to the 3rd century B.C. Availability of the text to the committee and loss of it thereafter indicates that the KJB is providentially accurate in places that modern versions can't be.

The KJB and LXX *mole* for the Hebrew *tinshemeth*, is contested by scholars favoring *chameleon*, but *mole* fits with the way Hebrews assigned names. Now *shrew* is the likely specific term here, but KJB translators simplified language for laymen, and a mole, related to a shrew, is more readily known to English readers (there's even an animal called a shrew mole), so the type of creature is rightly indicated by *mole*. *Tinshemeth* also applies to birds in Lev.11:18 and Dt.14:16, where it's rendered *swan* in the KJB, and the shrew and swan are related figuratively, justifying different renderings of *tinshemeth*. The root term of *tinshemeth* signifies angry puffing breath, and among birds in Leviticus and Deuteronomy, the swan, a graceful beautiful animal, hisses at adversaries, and *shrew* often signifies a graceful beautiful woman behaving as a hissing contentious person. A chameleon hisses but is far from beautiful or graceful. *Mole* (shrew) and *swan* are English terms suitable to represent Hebrew use of word pictures to assign names. *Swan* is in the Brenton LXX in the Leviticus/ Deuteronomy verses but in different order, suggesting corruption of original renderings that agreed with the KJB.

Scholars reject the KJB/LXX *chameleon*. They favor *monitor lizard* or *land crocodile*, but *chameleon* follows Hebrew naming. Hebrew *koach* here is often translated *power/strength*, but *ability* is a more-comprehensive meaning and applies to a chameleon more than other reptiles. It has ability to hide from predators, changing color to blend with foliage, ability to increase in size by air inflation to discourage predators and ability to snare insects instantly on its long tongue. Land crocodiles and monitor lizards have power, but no other notable ability.

Amplification in Aramaic Targumim

Targumim are Aramaic renderings of the Hebrew, paraphrased in variant degree and offering some commentary. Scholars think Jesus quoted such paraphrase, but use of the amplified Hebrew text is again indicated, that type of text being reflected in the targumim, and LXX, albeit to a lesser extent and in paraphrased form at times in targumim. A given passage may be dealt with by both, or only by one or the other. Targumim amplify Christology and emphasize Messianic interpretation of prophetic Hebrew-Text passages like Isaiah 53, Numbers 24:17 and Genesis 49: 10.[18] Regarding targumim longevity, as with the LXX-type texts, obsolescence-corruption would discredit them to prevent text competition with the Masoretic in the New Testament era.

Targumim passages reflecting an amplified textual basis
1. Isaiah 6:9,10 quoted by Christ at Mark 4:12.
a. Mk.4:12 in KJB: *That seeing they may see, and not perceive; and hearing they may hear, and not understand; lest at any time*

they should be converted, and their sins should be forgiven them.

b. Is.6:9,10 in the KJB Masoretic text: *And he said, Go, and tell this people, Hear ye indeed, but understand not; and see ye indeed, but perceive not...make their ears heavy, and shut their eyes; lest they see with their eyes, and hear with their ears...and convert, and be healed.*

The LXX is like the Masoretic, but both differ from Mark that expresses the healing as forgiveness of sin, and the latter is in an Isaiah targum.[18] The targum amplifies Isaiah to clarify that the type of healing intended is sin forgiveness characterizing Christ's ministry. The amplification culminates in the New Testament.

2. Mk.9:47,48 quotes Isaiah 66:24, speaking of *gehenna* hell-fire, while the Masoretic text and LXX speak of earthly fire. Mark's *gehenna* is from an Isaiah targum amplifying what earthly *fire* ultimately signifies here, eternal fire of the soul.[18] Amplification culminates in the New Testament to stress the ultimate result of rejecting Christ's very costly sacrifice for our salvation.

3. Lk.4:18 quotes Is.61:1, mainly with the LXX. But a final clause *to set at liberty them that are bruised* follows an Isaiah targum.[19] The targum amplifies the Masoretic *opening of the prison to them that are bound* to clarify the prison as that of sin that bruises.

Amplification Contained within the New Testament.

Some observations about "Joshua"
1. Jesus or Joshua gave rest to God's Old Testament people?
Christological amplification of Old Testament events can appear in the New Testament independent of other texts. The KJB Heb. 4:8, using His incarnate name Jesus, places Christ pre-incarnate in Israel's wilderness wandering of the exodus. This accords with Micah 5:2 that says He who entered the stream of human events at Bethlehem was eternal God *whose goings forth have been from of old, from everlasting* (no beginning of days - the modern version *ancient* in lieu of *everlasting* is mistranslation). Thus we

expect to see Him in theophany in the Old Testament. But most modern scholars reject Hebrews 4:8 as referring to Christ in the Old Testament, so the Christology here is missed today. [20]

In Heb.4:8 the KJB notes Jesus as not giving to most wilderness wanderers a spiritual rest in faith due to their lack of faith. Early-church elders indicated they understood the passage to refer to Christ,[18] but today scholars reject this since the Greek for Jesus (*Iesous*) corresponds to Joshua's Hebrew name (*Yeshua*). Scholars say the verse refers to historic Joshua who led his people to victories in Canaan. They say Joshua gave rest from warfare prefiguring greater spiritual rest of faith that God gives, so in Heb. 4:8, they view Joshua as giving physical rest, but not a final rest of faith.[21] They dismiss any suggestion of Christ in the passage.

In the New Testament, Greek forms of Hebrew names appear often, but that doesn't apply here. The Greek text is inspired, so *Iesous* in the Greek of the epistle can't be Joshua, for that creates identity confusion denying inerrancy, there being no qualifying explanation. If historical Joshua had been intended here, he'd be identified in a way other than a Greek transliteration of his name. This is very likely, for the scholarly Hebrews writer, an expert in Hebrew culture and Greek language, would see the ambiguity and the potential for misconstruing the Greek transliteration.

And the name Jesus in reference to Christ is noted shortly after verse 8, in verse 14, and the verse-8 theme on rest relates to the verse 14-16 theme on God's mercy and grace as the basis for rest. Indeed the name Jesus is noted in clear references to Christ throughout (2:9, 6:20, 7:22, 10:19, 12:2,24 & 13:12), but Joshua is nowhere evident and can't be abruptly introduced in 4:8.

The notion of Joshua in Heb.4:8 is linguistically and contextually unsound, as seen by more indication of Christ in Israel's past. The verse is preceded by an account in chapters 3,4 of failure of Moses-led wanderers to enter into a rest of faith in God. This spiritual rest is the type referenced in Heb.4:8, and the rest that

46

scripture associates Joshua with through his leadership in Canaan victories, was a physical temporal one. While Heb.4:8 implies the physical rest, it doesn't reference Joshua, for the physical rest was given by God through Christ, as seen by Christ appearing in theophany as *Captain of the Host* before whom Joshua bowed in submission before deciding Israel's actions (Jos.5:13-15). Thus even the implied physical rest refers to Christ, and it's this Jesus who didn't give the greater spiritual rest. Accordingly *he* in Heb. 4:8 refers to Christ, as expected with *Jesus* being the immediate grammatical antecedent to *he*, while modern versions link *he* to a grammatically-distant reference to God the Father.

With Christ as the giver of physical rest, language/context prove He is the Heb.4:7,8 Jesus. The KJB says...*he limiteth a certain day, saying in David, To day, after so long a time...harden not your hearts...if Jesus had given them rest* (implying the physical given by Christ preincarnate), *then would he not afterward have spoken of another day.* When *he* spoke of another day of rest, this was *in* or *through* David at the writing of Ps.95, ~400 years after the time of the historical Joshua. How can this Joshua be with the wilderness wanderers, and ~400 years later be alive and able to speak *in*, or through, David, speaking holy scripture? But the Lord Jesus Christ, the living eternal Word of God, has no trouble at all being with the wilderness wanderers, and 400 years later speaking through David in the writing of scripture.

NIV/RSV translators justified *Joshua* by changing *he* (God the Son) to *God* (the Father implied). This permits a change in passage sense that would allow the name *Joshua* linguistically (not contextually). But, as the RSV footnotes reveal, the word in the Greek is *he*, not *God*, and the NASV and Amplified, render *he*. The NASV tries to skirt the issue, capitalizing *H* in *he* to suggest God the Father or Jesus can be understood. Jewett [11] in a personal translation, with no group pressure, renders *he* and notes the impossibility that *Jesus* could be the historical Joshua.

The Hebrews writer relates Christ's role in dealing with lack of faith of God's Old Testament people at a time in history when the presence of Christ is verified in 1 Cor.10:4. Paul refers to Christ as the spiritual rock that followed Israel (under Moses in the wilderness wandering). A major purpose of the Hebrews writer is to relate Jesus, not Joshua, to Old Testament history, and Heb. 4:8 does so. He teaches Micah 5:2 truth on activities of Christ that pre-date His Incarnation at Bethlehem and illustrate that He is God without beginning of days.

2. Jesus or Joshua led God's Old Testament people? Another case of *Jesus* and Joshua is an Acts 7:45 confrontation of Stephen the Christian martyr with the Jerusalem council. In the KJB, Stephen speaks of Hebrew fathers bringing in the tabernacle <u>with Jesus</u> into Canaan. In the NASV and RSV, they bring in the tabernacle <u>with Joshua</u>, which is ambiguous and grammatically awkward; it can be interpreted logically as saying the fathers and Joshua brought in the tabernacle to Canaan, but can also be interpreted illogically as saying the fathers brought in Joshua and the tabernacle together. The problem is dealt with in the NIV by saying the tabernacle was brought in <u>under</u> Joshua's leadership, which is just incorrect paraphrase that simply obscures the issue and allows *Joshua*.

But *Jesus* offers dual-sense logic by amplification to suggest more than one truth and indicating *Jesus* is correct. This logic has physical and spiritual aspects. In a physical sense, the fathers act with Jesus, the Captain of the host and true leader, to bring in the tabernacle to Canaan. In a spiritual sense they bring in both the tabernacle and Jesus since the tabernacle is symbolic of Christ in several ways as any Pentateuch-class student knows.

The dual-sense logic is vital to Stephen who recounts Israel's history to show the council Jesus as the God of their history and denounce their crucifixion of Him (Acts 7:52). The council knows Jesus is Messiah (Mt.21:38) and can be convicted through scripture of their sin in betraying Him. And Stephen wouldn't miss the chance to stir up the council's scriptural knowledge, showing them the dual-sense logic of Jesus spiritually associated with the tabernacle and Captain of the Host (not Joshua) giving ancient Israel physical victories in Canaan. It would be Stephen's aim to show them that it was Jesus who gave the victories to correct their belief that Joshua did this. Thus he can't mean Joshua when he says *Jesus*, for this would defeat his intent. He must name Jesus the Christ openly at, or very near, the point of Acts 7:45 in his oration since he has only alluded to Him so far (Acts 7:37). The opportunity will soon be gone as he is very close to the point where he will denounce the council for betraying Jesus.

3. Abraham, Sarah and Isaac: Hebrews 11:11 Christological amplification in the New Testament includes a forerunner of the Virgin Birth in which Abraham's wife Sarah is said to conceive seed due to her faith, even though she's past child-bearing age. Traditionally Sarah has been seen as receiving enablement from God to conceive. Modern scholars struggle with the Greek here. They say it refers to enabling for a father's role in communicating seed for conception, not a mother's role in conceiving from the seed.[22] The NIV reflects this notion, changing the traditional rendering to make Abraham the one empowered through God's intervention for procreation in old age past the child-bearing stage. But this distorts passage sense, for Abraham's condition isn't the problem. Unlike women, men are never too old to father children, despite deadness of the body in this regard in old men. Sarah is the one in a hopeless condition for child-bearing. That Abraham isn't in need of intervention in this matter is seen in his fathering of children by Keturah after the death of Sarah (Gen. 25:1-2) and his fathering of Ishmael by Hagar just 13-14 years earlier (Gen.16:16). No suggestion of loss of ability to father children is seen in his history.

Sarah receives a miraculous enabling from God to conceive Isaac, and Abraham has nothing to do with the miraculous part of this conception. God passes on to Sarah something of Himself in the ability to bring life from that which is lifeless. God visited Sarah, not Abraham (Gen.21:1). Thus a suggestion in the Greek text of a father's role in the conception in this passage isn't that of Abraham, but is logically that of God the Father giving Sarah His power, or seed, of life. Abraham had no power to overcome Sarah's barrenness, and, even if he had been sterile, empowering him for procreation could not have produced children by barren Sarah, contrary to the NIV. Indeed Abraham's secondary role in the conception was not required to produce life from God's seed, but was permitted so that the miraculous birth would give typical offspring. Thus, as the KJB has it, Sarah, not Abraham, was the one enabled by God for procreation.

Hebrews 11 amplification reveals God enabling a woman so that Isaac's birth prefigured the Virgin Birth. The latter is far superior since here the human-father role was not only not required, but also not permitted, only the seed of life from God being involved here. Isaac's birth prefigures the Virgin Birth since both came to pass by God giving a woman the seed of life when normal human birth was impossible. The Virgin Birth achieves this while totally forbidding involvement of a man, so it's the fulfillment of the promise given by the prefiguring role of Isaac's birth.

Amplification in Heb.11:11 relates to Sarah's faith, and her faith is a matter further illustrating how scholars distort scripture interpretation with their opinion these days. They show no faith in the reliability of God's Word, so unlike ancients of the church who accepted the traditional understanding of Heb.11:11.[9] In their reasoning, scholars reject the traditional rendering due to their notion that Sarah isn't a fitting subject for the passage, Abraham being proposed in the NIV as the better subject. In the traditional rendering, Sarah is said to receive the ability to conceive through her faith in God. Scholars consider her a poor example of faith since she laughed when God, Christ pre-incarnate, informed her that she would have a child in her old age (Gen.18:9-15).

50

Heb.11:11 amplifies the nature of Sarah's laughter, showing her faith didn't fail and leading us to examine carefully Gen.18:9-15. The passage says Sarah very briefly laughed in her mind at the idea that one past the time of child-bearing could conceive. This would seem incredible to anyone in such a unique situation, who momentarily lost sight of the fact that it was God who promised. Sarah showed a lack of presence of mind, momentarily forgetting the ability of God and thinking only of the seeming impossibility of child-bearing in her. The brevity of this digression is revealed in the Genesis passage by the fear she immediately felt when she realized she had momentarily denied God's truth. Fear caused her to lie about laughing, illustrating her unstable thinking and her temporal emotional state in this situation. Great believers have moments of disbelief over circumstances requiring monumental faith, and this human limitation doesn't reflect on their established faith. Indeed such circumstances are the means by which their faith is made greater still. And the monumental degree of faith required in their latest challenge reveals the very advanced state of their present faith.

We see this when we remember Abraham too suffered a temporary lapse in presence of mind by laughing when God told him his wife would have a child in her old age. Understanding Sarah's reaction helps us understand his also, for like Sarah, he too recovered from his lapse in short order (Gen.17:15-27). In his earlier life, Abraham showed other temporary lapses of faith in not trusting God for physical protection. On two occasions he asked Sarah to say she was his sister to avoid harm to himself from those who might take her as a wife (Gen.12:12, 20:2).

It's important to realize that Abraham, like all believers, would go through a period of growth in faith, and this is reflected in the scriptures. His impropriety in not identifying Sarah as his wife in strange cities reflects an early immature faith (not trusting God for his safety). Considerable maturity of faith is seen in Gen.17: 15-27 where, despite his initial human skepticism over God's announcement of Sarah becoming a mother, he soon reacted in a way that proved his faith in God. As part of God's covenant with Abraham to make him a father whose seed by Sarah would be fruitful and blessed, God required Abraham to observe circumcision as his part in keeping of the covenant. In Gen.17:23-27 Abraham soon keeps the sign of the covenant among his entire household, so we see true faith evidenced in action, not just in words. What we see here is the true faithful nature of Abraham revealed shortly after temporary fleshly skepticism not yet fully dealt with as he grows in faith.

This situation brings to mind our Lord Jesus' parable on two sons told by their father to work in the vineyard (Mt.21:28-31). One son reacted quickly in immaturity by refusing, but soon showed his true colors when he repented and went to the field. This son, despite his initial wrong reaction, was said by the Lord to do the will of the father, by contrast with a second son who immediately said he would work in the vineyard, but never did.

When we realize the real Abraham is seen in his actions, not his initial verbal reply, we understand Paul in Rom.4:17-22 where he says Abraham believed God's promise that he and Sarah would have a son. Paul says Abraham didn't consider the deadness of his or Sarah's body and didn't stagger at the promise of God through unbelief. If we read this passage and Gen.17:15-27 carelessly, the two may seem contradictory. But that's not the case, for Paul rightly ignores Abraham's brief initial fleshly reply to God's promise since this wasn't characteristic of Abraham's true behavior, being just a human initial response to a promise of extraordinary nature. Paul deals with the true response of faith by the real (spiritual) Abraham evidenced in his action of faith in keeping the sign of the covenant. By his act of faith, Abraham, as Paul says, did not consider the deadness of his and Sarah's bodies and did not stagger at God's promise in unbelief, despite his brief initial response of skepticism. He just seemed about to do so, and that only very briefly since his faith wasn't yet developed enough to govern his fleshly initial reaction to a seemingly incredible promise. At this point he has come close to the faith that will one day make him the father, or precursor, of all the faithful in many nations of the world.

Well after the miraculous birth of Isaac we see Abraham in the full maturity of a faith so unswerving and automatic that he without question obeys God in an act that seemingly would take away his only true son he loved so dearly (Gen.22:2). He knows now that the God who gave him this miracle son under humanly impossible conditions can restore him from the dead if need be (Heb.11:19). It was at this late point in life that Abraham reached the zenith of faith, satisfying God's highest requirement of faith (Gen.22:12) that he might in every sense be a precursor, a father, of all believers whose mature faith pleases God (Rom.4:11).

Scholars are wrong to replace Sarah with Abraham in an epistle verse that reflects events at a point in time when even he wasn't fully mature in his faith. They can't rightly replace Sarah with Abraham in the Hebrews verse since his faith was no better than hers at that time. They would deprive Sarah of her place in scripture as a woman of outstanding faith on the basis of their opinion and poor grasp of Hebrews 11:11. In changing scripture they interfere with truth, as is ever their trend.

Non-Christological amplification in seemingly minor details
Jacob leans upon his staff in worshipping God: New Testament amplification involving a minor detail, appears in Heb.11:21 and Gen.47-48. Here New Testament amplification by clarification gives an important fuller understanding of Hebrew-text events. In Heb.11:21, Jacob is said to worship God as he leans upon his staff and blesses the sons of Joseph. Scholars say this refers to the LXX rendering of Gen.47:31 where Jacob, in requiring a vow of Joseph, bows himself upon his staff. But that would make Heb.11:21 contradict Gen.47:31, for in the Hebrew text, Jacob bowed himself upon the bed's head, not the staff of the LXX. Here the current LXX is corrupt, for it contradicts the Hebrew

text. The bed's head of Gen.47:31 is correct, and the Hebrews epistle doesn't refer to this. As has been noted, the reference can't be to 47:31, for Joseph's sons aren't present to be blessed in that passage.[14] The true Hebrew-text reference is Gen.48:1,2 where Jacob sits on his bed as he blesses Joseph's sons, there being no mention of the bed's head or a staff in the Hebrew text. Thus the Hebrews epistle, by providential guidance, reveals a hidden detail to complete the sense of the Hebrew-text Gen.48:1,2 passage. This detail is Jacob's leaning upon his staff for support to sit upright on his bed as he blesses Joseph's sons, as is proper for worship of God, so he sat on the edge of the bed. This fits the passage sense since Gen.48:2 in the Hebrew text says a weak Jacob strengthened himself to sit upon his bed, and the logical way he would do so is by use of a staff, the staff of Heb.11:21.

This minor amplification is quite significant. It reveals Jacob's worship of God as he prophesies blessings of God on Joseph's sons. This worship act was similar to his bowing on the bed's head in Gen.47:31 when he required a vow from Joseph before God. The worship established Jacob's blessings on Joseph's sons as prophecy that God would bring to pass, not mere wishful thoughts. Indeed scripture study shows these blessings of Jacob on Joseph's sons (Gen.48:16-20) were fulfilled in such things as Jacob's name (Israel) being conferred on Joseph's Egyptian sons, and the growth of the two sons into two great multitudes of people, and a greater prosperity of one (Ephraim) over the other (Manasseh) in Israel's history (Num.1:2,32-35; Jer.31:9,20 etc.)

Thus the Hebrews epistle shows us prophecy fulfilled by giving a small detail seemingly reserved for New Testament revelation. Actually the Hebrews epistle may be revealing a staff present in Gen.48 of an original LXX text, accidentally transferred to Gen.47:31 in the corrupt later LXX text. Thus amplification here may have originated in the original uncorrupted LXX.

New-Testament divergences from the LXX & Masoretic Text
Certain New Testament quotes of the Old don't fully reflect the LXX or Masoretic Text, suggesting to some that New Testament quotes can't always be harmonized with the Old Testament. But an amplified targum can be involved, as we noted earlier.

It's also been suggested that our Lord and His disciples at times improved corrupt LXX readings by making new Greek translations directly from the Hebrew text.[14,23] But Christ would quote an inerrant amplified LXX that He provided for His disciples. Amplification explains some seemingly-unique quotes of the Old Testament in the New, our Lord and His disciples quoting an original LXX-type text with amplification not in the standard Hebrew and not preserved in corrupt extant LXX texts. A New Testament quote will preserve an original, and its divergence from the Hebrew text will be due to amplification. Corruption in the current LXX text would include the deterioration of some amplification passages fully preserved in the New Testament or in authorized church-age Old-Testament translations.

Amplified-LXX Development

As noted, not only do the New Testament and LXX amplify the Old Testament, but later Old Testament books may amplify early ones. This explains some diversity among Old Testament texts that is orthodox, being supported by certain Masoretic books. Such diversity is providential amplification of teaching in the Old Testament era that advances or clarifies earlier scripture teaching to a degree. This doesn't conflict with preservation of a fixed standard scripture text throughout history. Amplification contributes to a history of progressive unveiling of the text, and originates prior to corruption processes in some texts. It's a stage in the history of unveiling of the standard text. In our view of orthodox diversity in the scripture text, we briefly review historic progressive unveiling of a fixed standard text.

Divine revelation, begun as verbal discourse with Adam, was in unwritten form until writing of the book of Job as early as 2000 B.C. (contrary to scholars). It continued with the law in the 15th century, followed by the Prophets and Writings concluding in the 5th century. The progression included New-Testament unveiling, concluding with the Revelation at the end of the 1st century A.D. Written revelation was unveiled over ~2100 years (scholars suggest a lesser time). Progression would include passages amplifying early scripture passages and providentially reiterating parts of God's revelation for timely deeper knowledge of past instruction, or new direction on past concepts. Amplification is progressively unveiled revelation given prior to closing of the canon with the New Testament. It's unique revelation having a role in progressive unveiling of the standard text, as verified by evidence.

The origin of amplification is initial standard-text books Job and Deuteronomy that added to early standard-text structure in minor fashion. Later, amplification would advance to include major parts of standard-text books, including fully-amplified books of Chronicles. Eventually the amplified Hebrew-Text edition that paralleled the standard text in 5th century B.C. Palestine, would provide a basis for the 3rd-2nd century B.C. LXX.

Factual basis for LXX amplification of the Masoretic Text
Amplification is clearly indicated by the Chronicles penned in the late 5th century B.C, after Babylonian exile. They relate much of the same information in 10th century B.C. Samuel and 6th century B.C. Kings, with abbreviation of basic material, plus added details. Such unique content of Chronicles would be a result of amplification, there being no other logical or orthodox reason to repeat Old Testament events with many added details. This is like the situation with the synoptic gospels that amplify each other with unique details to complete the picture of events, so the New Testament amplifies itself, in addition to the Old Testament, in fulfilling its role in finalizing amplification.

Prior to Qumran, scholars though the Chronicles penmen copied, and took liberties with, Samuel/Kings. But the Qumran Hebrew manuscripts (especially Samuel A) have the kind of text seen in Chronicles. The Chroniclers used a known Hebrew 5th-century B.C. text that amplified Samuel/Kings. At Chronicles this text contained new items basic to a 3rd-2nd century B.C. LXX Old Testament more notably different from the standard text and indicating progressive amplification. Thus canonical Masoretic Chronicles verify progressive amplification generating the fully unveiled standard text, and potentially developing further to generate a parallel amplified Hebrew text for an LXX-type text with extensive amplification of the standard Hebrew-text books.

The tie of Chronicles to the LXX and the Qumran Samuel A manuscript indicates that, in Samuel of the LXX, amplification parallels that of Chronicles. This is expected of an orthodox LXX Samuel since, with Samuel amplification being revealed in Chronicles, there is no other orthodox basis for an amplified Samuel in a parallel Hebrew-text edition.

Further evidence of the existence of an advanced amplified parallel Hebrew text for the LXX arises from finding a Qumran Hebrew manuscript giving Hebrew-text authority to the amplified LXX quotation of Dt.32:43 in Heb.1:6 of the New Testament (i.e. *Let all the angels of God worship him*). The New Testament is an inerrant resource preserving some original LXX renderings.

The length of an amplified Hebrew LXX-type text
Chronicles amplification would yield a short version of Samuel/ Kings. Details of many incidents in the earlier books would be omitted, there being no need to repeat everything to introduce amplification. An example is the shorter account of David's life in 1 Chronicles compared with that of 1 and 2 Samuel and 1 Kings. But in an LXX-type Hebrew text, the goal should be to reproduce events in the standard text with amplification of many incidents. This would result in a generally-expanded text in each book, as is often the case with the LXX. Yet abbreviation of some

details due to orthodox condensation like that of Chronicles is expected in a text that is for the purpose of amplification and need not preserve all details of the standard Text.

A proposed amplified LXX text development
Amplification appears in various standard books entering the canon after Deuteronomy, especially, The Writings. Chronicles and Psalms act as commentary amplifying Samuel/Kings, largely from David's viewpoint in Psalms. Proverbs, Ecclesiastes and Song of Solomon act as amplified poetic personal commentary from Solomon's view of his reign in Kings. Ezra, Nehemiah and Esther act as amplified prose imparting knowledge of post-exilic trials of Hebrews in Palestine and in the dispersion, due to disobedience to God. Lamentations acts as amplified commentary from Jeremiah's viewpoint, on Judah's woeful state in relation to the Babylonian conquest. Ruth acts as amplified commentary on hopeful matters for Israel during the trouble of the Judges period. The first Bible book, Job, qualifies as amplified poetic commentary on hardship that is part of the lifestyle of all God's people, concluding in a happy end, especially the ultimate end in the Messiah and the general resurrection (Job 19:25,26).

A substantially-amplified text introducing Chronicles as a step in the unveiling of a standard Hebrew Text would arise in the 5th century B.C. in Palestine. It would derive from manuscripts related to Ezra, the inspired author of the Ezra book and inspired traditional author of Chronicles. Historically, Ezra was assigned a role in text restoration in Judah after Babylonian exile (with assistance by many scribes and Great-Synagogue scholars, said to include Zechariah and Haggai, * tying Ezra to Messianic texts of these prophets). Ezra likely oversaw an amplified text that introduced Chronicles and other post-exilic books in the standard text, plus limited amplification of pre-exilic books. His authority would ensure acceptance of an amplified text by orthodox Jews

* Clarke, A. Clarke's Commentary. Introduction to the book of Ezra.

to avoid a view of amplification as corruption, such as Chronicles being viewed as a corrupt abbreviated Samuel/Kings.

An amplified text introducing Chronicles in the 5th-century B.C. would be a part of standard-text completion. Amplification later would motivate in the 5th-4th century B.C. a mildly-altered, non-authoritative Samaritan Pentateuch patterned after the standard Pentateuch. A fully developed amplified text continuing labors of Ezra et al, would be our parallel amplified Hebrew-text edition for the 3rd-2nd century B.C. LXX in Egypt. This amplification sequence helps explain why the LXX has many points of unique textual agreement with a Qumran Samuel A Hebrew manuscript related to Chronicles and the Samaritan Pentateuch, Chronicles and the LXX being related to a progressive amplified Hebrew text. This sequence can explain the dual text-type in standard temple manuscripts of Judea in the 2nd-1st centuries B.C,[24] the historic standard text being paralleled by an orthodox, amplified LXX-type Hebrew text by Ezra et al. from the 5th century B.C.

Amplification Development in the Masoretic Text

Amplification role in Masoretic books of post-exilic origin

Major amplification would be expected to begin in canonical books penned after the calamitous Babylonian captivity and exile, to increase emphasis on, and understanding of, the reasons for Judah's misfortune. This would be crucial since many would think that, after Assyrian captivity of the northern tribes, now God's plans for Judah had failed. The apparent failure included a seeming end of the eternal throne of David, loss of Judah's national identity and loss of a magnificent temple. And all this might seem to be through defeat of the true God by pagan gods of Babylon empowering king Nebuchadnezzar of Babylon.

But written revelation told the people their fortunes were in God's control, beginning with the unamplified books of Kings. Kings served to show the Babylonian Captivity was caused by disobedience to God, and periods of obedience brought blessing.

These books were likely penned in the 6th century B.C. during the captivity to encourage Judah to reflect on and understand the reasons for disaster. The Daniel book, written during, or shortly after, the captivity, served to show God's people that Babylon's gods had no role in Judah's defeat by Babylon. A helplessness of these gods against the true God is seen in the death of Belshazzar, the Babylonian king that succeeded Nebuchadnezzar, after he desecrated vessels of the Jerusalem temple in exalting his gods. The book of Daniel also showed God was with His captivity people in Babylon, as seen in the fiery-furnace deliverance of three faithful men from the wrath of Nebuchadnezzar, and later in Daniel's lion's-den victory over jealous rivals of the Medo-Persian empire that later conquered Babylon.

The Esther book, written about a century after captivity, showed God's people of the dispersion that He had not abandoned any of those scattered in exile, giving victory over enemies of those dispersed beyond Babylon (Esther and Mordacai were victorious over Haman in Shushan of the Medo-Persian empire).

Rebuilding of Jerusalem on return from Babylon, commencing in the late 6th century B.C, required assurance of God's will to deal with a sense of disaster for Judah. Post-exilic Chronicles, written in the 2nd half of the 5th century B.C, serves as an amplified review and interpretation of the past for all those returning to Jerusalem. Chronicles focuses on events of Samuel/Kings where trouble by disobedience is recorded, so Chronicles begins with a review of the history of people foundational to Israel, and ends by revealing captivity and rebuilding of Jerusalem as God's will (in the amplification sequence, Ezra and Nehemiah, extend this theme). This encourages reformation to restore God's blessing. Chronicles further fits this role in that it tends to emphasize hope for the future rather than despair from the past. In this regard it tends to omit failings of Judah's primary kings, like David's sin with Bathsheba and Solomon's later idolatry, and it concentrates on more positive aspects of the past that must accompany Judah's efforts to be obedient. Notably, it reveals something not in the Kings account of Solomon's prayer of temple dedication, fire from heaven (2 Chron.7:1-3) to emphasize God's acceptance of the kind of consecration seen early in Solomon's reign, which Judah had to focus on after captivity. Chronicles tends to ignore idolatrous kings of Israel, focusing on the more orthodox kings of Judah, as expected if faithfulness to God in a rebuilt Jerusalem is a key aim of Chronicles. Chronicles emphasizes the orthodox temple order, recognizing a need for Old Covenant reformation.

Form of amplification in Masoretic books of later origin
Chronicles/Samuel/Kings: We can profitably engage in study of Samuel, Kings and Chronicles to see if amplification explains the differences between Chronicles and Samuel/Kings in parallel passages and thus accounts for new information in Chronicles.

The general purpose of amplification would be to complete a partial message in an early book. Limited repetition with addition of amplifying material encourages study of God's Word through cross-referencing, an approach well suited for readers who, having learned the folly of disobedience, desire to know all that God would teach them. Chronicles amplification advances knowledge of Old Testament concepts for emphasis in hindsight on lessons of scripture still having application for God's Old Covenant people at their time in history (as with Nehemiah and Ezra). But lessons from the past are helpful in avoiding mistakes in the future, and we expect a futuristic aspect. In Chronicles, futurism is short term, reformation being in accord with Old Testament principles. Some futurism with a long-term aspect is found in other Masoretic books of pre-exilic origin with amplification for the approaching Christian era as God's plan for His people takes a new direction, but one building on Old Testament foundations (amplified books of Haggai, Zechariah and Malachi).

Another general purpose of amplification is fulfillment of themes begun in earlier books, and in this regard the reader should study other Old Testament books appearing in the canon after Babylonian exile. They, with Chronicles, constitute an amplified post-exilic portion of the standard text. Some are, like Chronicles, backward-looking books aimed at Old-Covenant reformation, but amplify general themes instead of textual detail amplified in Chronicles. In this regard post-exilic Nehemiah and Ezra books amplify a lesson on the cost of past disobedience, showing that the cost continues in the opposition and hardship Judah must face even as it attempts rebuilding and Old Covenant reformation.

A final answer to the trouble is seen in forward-looking New-Testament type revelation in post-exilic books Haggai, Zechariah and Malachi where forward-looking amplification answers problems noted in earlier books. All three books are prophetic with a Messianic tone, and this prophecy is amplification relating the past to the future. Haggai briefly introduces a renewed Messianic hope on return from Babylon, and Zechariah enlarges much on the nature of Messiah's ministry. Malachi, terminology is indicative of an imminent failure of Judah at Old Covenant reformation and the advent of Christ to provide the ultimate way of righteousness, and detail beyond this carries the reader further into the future. In these books, futuristic amplification points to Christ of a New Jerusalem as the real means by which the eternality of David's throne and Judah's kingdom and its true temple will be secured (Rev.21), despite temporal failure of the earthly throne, kingdom and temple before the power of Babylon seen in earlier books. Malachi appears even to predict the end of Judah's opportunity for reformation under the Old Covenant and ordination of the New Testament. This book has unmistakable terminology about a new Elijah (John the Baptist) and the *Sun of Righteousness* (Christ) in a perfect fulfillment of God's law. Malachi stipulates fiery judgment for refusal of the righteousness of this final offer (Mal.3-4), and seems to be ultimate futuristic amplification, revealing where real hope lies and warning the future Judah not to reject this final deliverance. Zechariah,

Haggai and Malachi can be seen as amplifying general themes of Masoretic books of an earlier origin, offering New-Testament resolution of old problems that incurred God's anger, like idol-worship, unconsecrated service and unworthy sacrifices.

Amplification in the standard text is most applicable to post-exilic Chronicles, but includes other books. Like Deuteronomy, various books show minor amplification, but don't build in major ways on textual detail of earlier books, so they don't repeat much detail and of course don't require a separate text. They introduce a text of mainly new content with minor earlier detail. Psalms is notable in this way, including some minor detail from other books. Minor amplification should be possible in any book that was introduced after the Pentateuch, and perhaps the first four Pentateuch books alone have none. Amplification is the least in Deuteronomy. The need for, and likelihood of it, should be least in early books, so it's no surprise that scholars consider the Masoretic Pentateuch to be nearly free of expansion (their view), and the Pentateuch to be the least expanded part of the LXX. Job is the earliest book, but it utilizes a little amplification since it encompasses the lifestyle of all who would be God's people.

And forward-looking amplification appears in pre-exilic Masoretic books. Psalms and Isaiah illustrate this, as seen by examples of amplification given earlier. Psalms is notable in this, for David is associated with Christ prophetically and through Joseph and Mary. The association wasn't understood in the Old Testament era, but it established the legitimacy of Christ's claim of being the Son of David and the ultimate heir to David's throne.

Examples of Chronicles' amplification of national history
Chronicles is clearly written for amplification purposes. Many passages show amplification of likely providential design, and some are noted below. Scholars think some parallel passages of Chronicles and Samuel/Kings are contradictory. We view them from a perspective of Chronicles amplifying Samuel and Kings.

1. Amplification of God's will is seen in the last two verses of 2 Chronicles in the proclamation of Cyrus, King of Persia, who ruled captive Hebrews after Babylonian rule was overthrown. In these unusual verses, Cyrus reveals he has been moved by God to give freedom to Judah to rebuild the temple at Jerusalem. In reading this passage with its proclamation by the pagan king, Judah would see plainly that God rules in all things and that the captivity experience and the subsequent release were ordained of God. Judah should also see from this that a new obedience to God must mark rebuilding and reordering of the nation.

2. The extensive genealogy in much of 1 Chronicles that extends from Adam is not found elsewhere in Samuel or Kings and can be for a unique amplification purpose. It appears to be a great passing-in-review of the entire cast of past members comprising the great plan of God for His people over the centuries. It shows that God's plan for His people hasn't been frustrated, their station and chronology in the nation's history being carefully preserved and ordained of Him. This shows they should never lose their sense of purpose, as they can be restored to His favor and secure their future in His plan anytime they are ready to be obedient.

3. Emphasis on God's written Word would be central to renewed dedication to obedient service, and this will appear in Chronicles if amplification of God's will is intended. Such emphasis is in 2 Chron.17:9 in the reign of good king Jehoshaphat and is not found in a 2 Kings parallel passage, indicating amplification of this principle in Chronicles. Great good that came to Jehoshaphat in ensuing verses of Chronicles 17 seems to be associated with the teaching of the biblical book of the law to the people.

The importance of knowing and keeping the Word of God is emphasized in both Chronicles and Kings. In the rule of the last good King of Judah, Josiah, the lost book of the law was re-covered, and an attendant great blessing followed for Judah one last time before the Babylonian disaster fell.

4. The patience of God with the failings of His people is evident in both Kings and Chronicles as He restores them each time after transgressions. It is important for Judah to reflect on, and grasp, this firmly in captivity by knowing Kings, and to exercise this knowledge as they go forward from rebuilding of Jerusalem by knowing Kings and Chronicles. New leaders are to understand improper aspects of bad leadership in error like worship of false gods and trusting in strong men rather than God. Thus Kings and Chronicles are God's vital provision of guidance for the captivity and post-captivity periods of Judah's history.

Chronicles gives amplification for deeper understanding of details on problems noted in Samuel/Kings. For example, in 2 Kgs.16 evil king Ahaz of Judah is beseiged (but not overcome) by Rezin king of Syria and Pekah king of Israel (Samaria). He sends to the King of Assyria for help using silver and gold in the temple and his own house as tribute. The king of Assyria delivers Ahaz, but association with the king causes Ahaz to add an altar of false worship to the temple. Amplifying information on the reign of Ahaz is given in a parallel passage in 2 Chron.28. This verse adds detail on the siege of Judah noted in Kings, telling us that, while Ahaz wasn't overcome in this siege, many inhabitants of Judah were killed or carried off by Syria and Israel as a consequence of bad leadership by Ahaz. This provides knowledge of the harm done by bad leadership even when things seem not all that bad in general. From Chronicles we also learn that those carried off by Israel were later released as part of revelation from God that Israel was not to mistreat its brethren of Judah, despite the hostility between them and despite God's chastising of Judah. This provides Judah with new understanding to guide exercise of brotherhood in the rebuilt Jerusalem.

Chronicles reveals a second siege not in Kings, again by two foes at once, Edomites and Philistines. Again Ahaz calls on the king of Assyria, instead of God, for help, and again he sends tribute to Assyria. Now he receives no assistance from the fed-up king and instead is distressed by Assyria, as well as Edom and

Philistia. Troubles multiply when Judah's leadership persists in disobedience. We also learn here in Chronicles that, during his troubles with neighboring countries, Ahaz had sacrificed to gods of Syria, to receive help from the powers he supposed had earlier brought on him the wrath of Syria. Of course this illustrates how wrong it is to imagine false gods have anything to do with the destiny of God's people, as the Book of Daniel taught. Thus the Chronicles passage amplifies the Kings passage to illustrate the full depth of the depravity of Ahaz and a resultant extreme plight of Judah and to give other details vital to Judah's future.

5. In 2 Chron.28:17, we learn Edomites had attacked Judah in the past, and the mention of Edomites is important in understanding all that the reign of Ahaz is to teach to Judah. First we note that in 2 Kgs.16:6 during the first siege of Judah, Syrians under Rezin, king of Syria, recovered a former possession from Judah, the city of Elath in Edom. Scholars think mention of Syria here is an error, thinking it had to be Edomites who were attacking Judah in Kings to recover their own city, but that's wrong. Rezin is identified as king of Syria reigning at Damascus and involved in the first siege of Judah in Isaiah 7,8 & 9. Isaiah 7 notes the first siege in which Rezin and Pekah don't prevail against Ahaz, confirming that Syrian-led forces under Rezin took Elath in the first siege. And Isa.9:11-12 notes the second siege where it refers to <u>Syria</u> and the Philistines as those attacking Judah, in contrast with the 2 Chronicles 28 note on <u>Edom</u> and Philistines as the aggressors. Chronicles amplifies Kings, showing that Syria and Edom refer to the same aggressors so that the 2 Kgs.16:6 note on Syria is correct. What scripture teaches in Isaiah and information from the Chronicles and Kings passages is that Edom was a possession of Syria so that Edomites were Syrians by military conquest and served Syria at this time.

This Syria/Edom alliance is further proved by earlier history in 2 Sam.8:13,14 and 1 Chron.18:12,13. In 2 Sam.8:13 David smites 18,000 Syrians in the Valley of Salt (in Edom), and immediately following in verse 8:14 he is said to establish garrisons in Edom. In 1 Chron.18:12,13 the same incidents are related in the same order, and the 18,000 Syrians slain by David in the Valley of Salt are called Edomites, showing through amplification they were Edomites who were also Syrians by military conquest and occupation of their land. Amplification here also tells us David's slaying of 18,000 in the Valley of Salt was figurative, being literally done by his general Abishai.

By Chronicles amplification we deduce that Elath, a crucial Edomite seaport in the south of Edom (the only seaport access to the east and used by Solomon earlier), was at one time under Syrian control. David evidently took it away from Syria so that Solomon enjoyed benefits of ownership. But evidently it was lost again and had to be restored again to Judah by king Amaziah's son Azariah (2 Kgs.14:22). Amaziah perhaps began recovery of Elath in his exploits of 2 Kgs.14:7 as he imitated conquests of David by slaying 10,000 Edomites in the Valley of Salt. Then in the still later reign of the evil king Ahaz, Judah again lost Elath to Edom, and thus to Syria, as noted in 2 Kings 16:6.

Thus Chronicles background amplification gives incidental information proving 2 Kgs.16:6 is correct in calling those who recovered Elath Syrians, Edomites under Syrian king Rezin, recovering Elath for their conqueror Syria. The misfortune of Edom here is evident in that their earlier conquest by Syria would cost them blood and servitude, and in battling Israel to reclaim Elath for their Syrian conquerors, they would again pay this price.

As a consequence of all this, in the Chronicles passage Judah has a permanent inerrant record that shows how truly calamitous the reign of Ahaz was. Chronicles shows two besiegements by multiple enemies involving loss of many captives and shows the entry of false worship into the land. It also shows economic disaster in that Judah lost the only seaport lifeline for trade with the East. It also shows how the misery of disobedient Edom under conquering Syria emphasized disobedient Judah's disaster. Full understanding of these events is intended for those who, knowing the disaster arising from ignoring God's Word, desire to know it in the fullest to realize full benefit from it.

6. The final end of Ahaz wasn't a place of honored burial with former kings, but we're not told this in 2 Kings where Ahaz is just said to have slept with his fathers (died) and was buried in Jerusalem. In the amplified 2 Chron.28:27, we see that while he was buried in Jerusalem, he wasn't given an honored place in the sepulchres of kings. Chronicles amplification depicts a sorry end of bad leadership to provide Judah with leadership lessons.

7. A unique amplification on the manner in which God manifests His wrath is seen in comparison of 2 Samuel 24 and 1 Chronicles 21 that suggest to scholars a contradiction in scripture. In the Samuel verse, God is said to move David in a way that brought judgment on Israel, while in Chronicles satan is said to be the one that moved David. Actually we see two different aspects of one judgment mechanism. In the Samuel passage God is angered by a certain unspecified aspect of Israel's behavior, and He works through David to bring judgment on Israel in a way that causes David to number Israel's human strength. Numbering is wrong since it is indicative of trusting in man rather than God, but God allows this for judgment of other sin in Israel. But it seems improper to ascribe to God allowance of an evil action, and we wonder how this can be reconciled with God's holy nature. The answer is that this is a case of God's permissive will in which He moves David by removing His hand of protection from Israel which results in judgment since the unavoidable result is that satan will wreak havoc on David and Israel. We can't see this in the Samuel passage alone which reveals only that God brings about the judgment. But we see it if we add new information in the amplified passage of 1 Chronicles 21 where we learn in verse 1 that it is satan who personally induced David to number Israel that judgment determined by God might fall on Israel. The Chronicles verse shows strong evidence of amplification in that Satan's name appears, which is uncommon in the Old Testament.

8. In 2 Sam.24 and 1 Chron.21 David builds an altar to sacrifice to God for his very costly sin causing the deaths of 70,000 men of Israel. 1 Chron.22 says the site of David's altar will become the site of Israel's temple. Chronicles amplification reveals that God brings good from even disastrous situations, this being important to encourage Judah after the Babylonian captivity.

9. 2 Chron.22:2 notes the age of evil king Ahaziah of Judah. He is said to be 42 years old when he begins his reign in Judah at the death of his father. Scholars speak of a contradiction since in the parallel 2 Kgs.8:26 passage, Ahaziah is said to be 22 years old as he begins to reign. He clearly was literally 22 years old at the start of his reign since, in 2 Chron.21:20 and 2 Kgs.8:17, Jehoram his father (can also be called Joram, an equivalent variant) is said to be 32 at the start of his reign and he reigns 8 years before his death so that his age at death was 40. Clearly Ahaziah can't be literally 42 years old at the start of his reign at the death of his father since that would make him 2 years older than his father.

But even those who reject inerrancy can't say the 42-year age figure is an error, for it appears in 2 Chron.22:2 in just the second verse after the 40-year age of Ahaziah's father at death appears in 2 Chron.21:20. Thus neither the original writer nor a copyist could misunderstand the literal inaccuracy of the 42-year age figure due to the so-recent note on his father's age that makes any such error obvious. And miscopying the age in Chronicles is very unlikely, for the numeral forms are very different. Even if short-form characters for 20 and 40 were involved, mistaking the two is unlikely since they too are notably different in form.

What then is the meaning of the 42-year age in 2 Chron.22: 2? We suspect Chronicles presents more of the amplification it often exhibits, the 42 years not being a literal age, but a figurative one representing some period of time related to Ahaziah. A figurative age is actually used here, in relation to the close link of Ahaziah king of Judah and Joram king of Israel.

Ahaziah's father is usually called Jehoram, distinguishing

him from Israel's king, usually called Joram, though these are different forms of one name. Close ties were forbidden by the Lord, as Israel in the north was idolatrous, and Judah in the south had to remain separate from compromised brethren to preserve its loyalty to God. But Ahaziah began what likely was the closest ecumenical tie of Judah to idolatrous Israel in their history. Joram of Israel and Ahaziah's father Jehoram were closely allied since the latter had married Athaliah, daughter of former king Omri of Israel whose son Ahab was the most idolatrous king in Israel's history. Joram of Israel and Ahaziah's father had the same name, being so alike in character, and Ahaziah of Judah had the same name as the brother of Joram of Israel who ruled Israel before Joram. Total character interrelationship is reflected in the names. Scripture even seems to abruptly interchange the names of Joram and Jehoram, possibly to show they're so closely linked that one is considered as if he were the other (2 Kgs.8:21, 24 & 2 Chron.22:5,7), though this isn't unique to these passages.

In 2 Kgs.8:27-29 we learn Ahaziah followed his father's bad example in marrying into the house of Ahab and cooperated freely with the king of Israel in military campaigns. Ahaziah's total acceptance of the ways of Ahab is seen as amplification in 2 Chron.22:3,4 shows us his mother and others of the house of Omri/Ahab (likely including his wife) were his counselors in evil endeavor. We learn in 2 Kings 8 that when Joram of Israel was wounded in battle by the Syrians, Ahaziah went to visit him as he recovered in Jezreel. In the 2 Chron.22:6-7 parallel passage, amplification tells us that Ahaziah's visit to Joram at Jezreel is a matter of God's will that will result in Ahaziah's death at the hand of Jehu who is about to kill Joram and rule Israel. Thus through amplification we see the logical end of a life given over to disobedience to God and misleading of the people of Judah.

Ahaziah's figurative 42-year age is amplification for edification on ecumenism. He's totally disobedient to God, fraternizing with idolaters and so closely tied to them his life blends with theirs in personal matters and business (military business). His life ends at the same time, in the same place, by the same people and, as we will see, in the same way, in poetic justice. He is inseparably linked with Joram of Israel and the idolatrous house of Ahab, and he perpetrates the spirit of Ahab on Judah and fully identifies Judah with Israel. Thus the reign of Ahaziah extends the reign of Jehoram of Judah and his cohort Joram of Israel, who, together and separately, perpetrated the spirit of Ahab in Judah. Two evil leaders allied in endeavors and having the same name, influenced Judah several years before Ahaziah reigned. Ahaziah's reign will continue this bad leadership. In assigning a figurative age to Ahaziah at the beginning of his reign, Chronicles stresses that Ahaziah's reign will be business as usual of a foul nature. As he comes to the throne, he is already old figuratively, representing continuance of the spirit of Ahab that has badly influenced Israel and Judah for 41 years and will do so for one more year until Ahaziah dies, so he's assigned a figurative 42-year age, prophesying his death within a year. This sums up, at his death, the total time of the reign in Israel of the spirit of Ahab, Israel's most idolatrous king and the time of this influence on Judah. God is saying, Ahaziah's reign is already over even as it begins.

This reasoning is likely, as seen by Ahaziah's tie with Israel, beginning with Omri, a king of Israel responsible for unusual evil influence, later tied to his son Ahab. That the 42 years is the time of the rule of the spirit of Ahab is indicated in that 2 Chron.22:2 says, *A son of 42 years,*[25] which, though it's common Hebrew language, likely signifies here, a son of a 42-year period of the spirit of Ahab in Israel and Judah. This period is outlined below.

After the house of Jeroboam was destroyed for bringing rampant idolatry to Israel, that line ended. Omri was elected by the army as Israel's king in response to Zimri's coup effort at Tirzah. Omri beseiged Tirzah and ousted Zimri but didn't secure his reign at Tirzah, which had broken into two camps, one under Tibni. After a 4-year struggle with Tibni's army (compare 1 Kgs.16:15 and

16:23), Omri began ruling there. After 6 years of rule at Tirzah, Omri prevailed and began 6 more years of uncontested rule, now at Samaria. This latter 6-years of respite from war was evidently when Omri committed idolatry worse than that of Jeroboam, so for 6 years an unusual spirit of worsening rebellion against God occurred, and this spirit came to be fully identified with Omri's son Ahab, Israel's most idolatrous ruler, who ruled 22 years. This spirit continued with Ahab's son Ahaziah who ruled 2 years. Ahaziah died without a son and was succeeded by his brother Joram (or Jehoram - 2 Kgs.1:17). The latter had ruled Israel for 11 years at the time of the death of king Jehoram of Judah and for 12 years at his own death (2 Kgs.3:1). Thus when the reign of Ahaziah of Judah began at the death of Jehoram of Judah, one year before the death of Joram of Israel, the spirit of Ahab had reigned in Israel since halfway through the reign of Omri 41 years ago (6 + 22 + 2 + 11). This spirit had influenced Judah for 41 years, controlling Ahaziah's father Jehoram for 8 years. Earlier it influenced Jehoram's father, good king Jehoshaphat, who during his 25-year rule of Judah (2 Chr.19:2), helped idolatrous Ahab in military matters, contrary to God's will (1 Kgs.22). He cooperated with Israel's evil king Ahaziah in trade operations (2 Chron.20:35-37 amplifies 1 Kgs.22:48-49, the latter showing he balked at cooperation, but Chronicles tells us he cooperated before balking). It also appears the spirit of Ahab influenced Jehoshaphat's father, good king Asa, who ruled Judah for 41 years prior to Jehoshaphat and in the latter part of his reign imitated Israel's tendency to trust in man rather than God (2 Chron.16:2-13 & 1 Kgs.15:17-20). Thus there was a progressive evil influence on Judah by the house of Ahab, ending in Ahaziah who likely would have outdone his father as the worst ecumenist in Judah's history.

But ecumenism will soon end. Ahaziah's 42-year figurative age signifies the time God will tolerate Judah's kings corrupting the nation by the spirit of Ahab. By amplification God's Word proclaims the sum of the years of His patience with ecumenical influence. The 2 Chron.22 passage indicates Ahaziah will reign just one year in Judah and will die with Joram of Israel, pointing to an approaching end of this foul leadership representing the spirit of Ahab. At his death in 2 Chron.22:10-11, his house ends by the hand of his mother Athaliah who kills all heirs but one she overlooks who is needed to keep the line intact. We see in 2 Kgs. 10 the end of the male kingly line of the house of Omri/Ahab at the hand of Jehu. With the end of Ahaziah's reign, God ends the rule of Judah's kings temporarily and allows a 6-year period of rule by Athaliah, daughter of Omri and of Israel's idolatry who is not at all a king. Her rule is likely meant to give Judah a final un-mitigated dose of the spirit of Ahab it had tolerated so long since her 6 years equal the 6 of Omri who began the period of trouble.

Chronicles amplification shows ecumenism causes inseparable identity of God's people with His enemies in extreme cases and destruction with the enemies. This contrasts with 1 Chron.18:12 where amplification showed that those who follow God's will (Abishai & David) are inseparably linked. Perhaps the figurative Chronicles 42-year age is more far-reaching than our passage. God may be warning against ecumenical associations of His peo-ple in all eras. The New Testament teaches this (2 Cor.6:14-18).

A further detail about Ahaziah concludes the amplification role in Chronicles. His death is described differently in 2 Kgs.9:27 and 2 Chron.22:9, and the two verses must be combined to see just how the king died. When Ahaziah sees Joram killed by an arrow while fleeing in his chariot, he flees in his chariot, but Jehu intends to mete out to him the same fate that befell Joram.

2 Kings

9:27 *But when Ahaziah the king of Judah saw this, he fled by the way of the garden house. And Jehu followed after him, and said, Smite him also in the chariot. And they did so at the going up to Gur, which is by Ibleam. And he fled to Megiddo, and died there.*
9:28 *And his servants carried him in a chariot to Jerusalem, and buried him...*

22:9 And he sought Ahaziah: and they caught him, (for he was hid in Samaria,) and brought him to Jehu: and when they had slain him, they buried him.

In the Kings account Ahaziah flees while Jehu's men follow, and he is mortally wounded near Ibleam located southwest of Jezreel where he and Joram had met. He eventually reaches Megiddo many miles to the northwest of Ibleam, and he dies there. Thus he died from an arrow delivered while in his chariot, just as Joram died, for a sword or spear wound would be at close range, and Ahaziah wouldn't then be able to stay ahead of his pursuers on to Megiddo still many miles away. Ahaziah's death paralleled that of Joram fully, as his life did, and poetic justice was served.

From the Chronicles account, we learn that, during his flight Ahaziah eluded his pursuers for a time, continuing on in a south-western direction from Ibleam and on to Samaria where he hid for a time before being discovered by his pursuers. After this he turned in a northwestern direction in his flight and reached Megiddo before dying of his earlier arrow wound. This shows us he sought refuge in the capital city of the nation whose idolatrous leadership he had cooperated with in exalting the spirit of Ahab (Jezreel was another city of the king's dwelling). But he found no refuge and was left to his unavoidable fate. He had much time to consider the error of his ecumenical ways as he desperately fled from his unrelenting pursuers and his life slowly ebbed away.

Continuing with Chronicles, Ahaziah is returned to Jehu (dead). Here events in Chronicles are not in chronological order, mention of the slaying and burial following that of the return of Ahaziah. Such expression is a result of a later event offered for emphasis before a final summary of events. Jehu's verification of Ahaziah's capture (dead) is emphasized, and is followed by a parenthetical phrase briefly summarizing the overall event.

The Chronicles passage ends with Jehu's soldiers burying Ahaziah, and from the Kings passage, we see that the way they did so was to allow Ahaziah's servants to do so. This is like the expression, "We bury the dead out of respect for human dignity." We don't necessarily do so personally, but encourage the practice. This is the case here, Chronicles saying Jehu's party "buried" Ahaziah (allowed his burial) in recognition of the fact he was a descendant of good king Jehoshaphat. This contrasts with Jehu's treatment of Jezebel, whose body was trampled in the street of Jezreel and eaten of dogs. Her fate is different, likely because as Ahab's wife and daughter of an idol-worshipping king, she turned Ahab to idol-worship, slew God's prophets (1 Kgs.16:30-33, 18:13) and slew innocent Naboth for property rights (1 Kgs.21).

What Do You Do with an Extra Orthodox Hebrew Text?

Earlier amplified books would cause no text confusion since they became part of the standard text. But a parallel edition of the standard text had to be subjected to a later obsolescence process to prevent competition with the Masoretic-Text intended for sole authority as the finalized Old Testament. Resultant disharmony would discourage active use by God's people to ensure against confusion. The obsolescence mechanism would be revision by men due to corruption suggested by contrasting amplified and unamplified texts. The men would be of late enough generations to lose touch with an orthodox origin of the amplified LXX-type of text in Ezra, not realizing the standard text had developed in part from a text of more limited amplified nature. Included would be Palestinian Jews confused over different 2nd-1st century B.C. temple standard Hebrew text-types.

Also included would be Hellenist Jews of the 2nd century B.C. and later, those knowledgeable of the LXX and the standard text. Some would know LXX origins by inexact tradition and defend it while respecting the Hebrew standard. Thus apparent debate over the need for LXX revision in Hellenist Alexandria induced, probably in the 2nd century B.C., the famous letter of Aristeas in defense of the LXX and later supportive defenses of Hellenist Jews Philo and Josephus. A contest would arise from efforts to retain the orthodox amplified LXX against pressure to accept a revised text returning to conformity with an ancient standard. This would be Providential, LXX defenders promoting truth in an original text undergoing obsolescence so later generations might know about its role, while antagonists advanced the ordained obsolescence process. Earlier amplified passages would be preserved in later books, and LXX-amplified passages would be preserved in the New Testament and in select Old Testament translations before obsolescence preceded without hindrance.

Planned LXX obsolescence
The New Testament finalizes revelation to complete and fulfill mystery and partial revelation in the Masoretic Text. Masoretic and Greek Received texts are the final aim, and the LXX and its basis had to be subjected to obsolescence to avoid competition. And the LXX could blur distinctions between the Old and New Testaments to make Christ less veiled in the Old, and the New seem less like the final revelation that it is. Obsolescence could be enacted since amplified passages were preserved elsewhere.

Thus the LXX and its Hebrew basis would undergo removal of divine preservation. The unavoidable result was a natural great uncertainty and disharmony like that in LXX texts today. The Vaticanus and Sinaiticus texts exhibit such disharmony that even monumental efforts to recover the original text have been very unsuccessful.[26] Errors in all extant LXX texts are many. The restraining hand of Providence has allowed modern readers to see amplification still present that men of faith might have evidence by which to understand the matter and adhere to faith on the basis of logic. LXX errors include amplification imitations in the form of apocrypha and pseudepigrapha purported to expand scripture by men's insight. It seems likely that scribes of ancient days recognized text amplification and imitated it.

Occurrence of LXX-type text obsolescence not long after New Testament completion is evident in severe corruption of the most prized extant LXX manuscripts, penned after New Testament completion at the end of the 1st century A.D. LXX corruption marked a general end of its usefulness to the church by the 4th century at the latest, and likely earlier. LXX manuscripts that scholars value most, 4th-5th century uncials Vaticanus, Sinaiticus and Alexandrinus[27] are very discordant among themselves.[26,28,29] Extant LXX manuscripts include incomplete fragmentary texts of manuscripts dating from the 3rd and 2nd centuries A.D.[30] A few LXX-scroll fragments have Pentateuch verses as old as the 1st and 2nd centuries B.C.[27,29] Perhaps revision began very early in text history,[27] and earliest fragments may be parts of revisions closer to the original than the corrupt current text. Obsolescence may have begun in limited degree before the Church age, being rampant after completion of the New Testament. If so, it would be needful for Christ to identify to the church LXX manuscripts representing the original text. The concept of pre-church LXX revisions offers a good reason for the requirement of apostolic authority in accepting any text in the New Testament canon, that Christ would show His apostles which manuscripts had original LXX-type renderings to be quoted in their writings.

Obsolescence of LXX-type texts was realized notably in the case of Vaticanus, Sinaiticus and Alexandrinus that, by the 5th century had fallen into disuse in churches, effectively lasting until the 19th century. Inclusion of apocrypha as an integral part of the Old Testament text in such manuscripts would be part of the obsolescence plan to motivate abandonment of them by churches (the original LXX would exclude apocrypha). But most of the organized church preferred the LXX, despite corruption like non-canonical apocrypha, which should have ensured text rejection. Apocrypha weren't rejected as scripture in large measure until the Reformation. The inerrant canonical Hebrew text was lost to the early church and wasn't widely restored until the dawn of the Reformation era when biblical guidance was widely renewed. Jerome had unsuccessfully attempted restoration in the western church in the early fifth century.

Scholars prefer New-Testament texts added to corrupt LXX texts and thus even further along in the corruption process, using them as a basis for modern-version New Testaments. There is even a new fascination with apocrypha by scholars, likely due to their love of the unorthodox in the rampant apostasy of our age.

In view of the historic failure to abandon the LXX, God might give the church a reliable LXX text to preserve Old Testament truth temporarily before the wide return of the canonical Hebrew text in the Reformation era (Jerome's Vulgate Old Testament from the Hebrew included apocrypha integral to the text, against his wishes, plus other variance from the Hebrew text).

Obsolescence need not include all manuscripts, and reliable representation of the original text could continue in manuscripts of biblical churches in pre-Reformation times. There's no way to know this with all the discord in extant LXX manuscripts, which may reflect how Providence arranges such matters. Today there's no real alternative to adherence to the Masoretic Text, which is likely intended by Providence. There are clues to the identity of an original LXX, which is likely also the intention of Providence.

Ongoing provision of an accurate LXX text is suggested in church history. The 2nd-century A.D. Old Latin Bible suffered obsolescence, likely because it retained the LXX Old Testament, but there's a suggestion that this version preserved truth in some manuscripts. Augustine testified to this in his note around the beginning of the 5th century on an Old Latin text-type variously known as the Italic, Itala or Italian, that was still reliable, while other Old Latin texts showed extensive corruption. [29]

Topic B End Notes

1. J. Rast. Jan. 2006 *The Coming War of Gog and Magog, An Islamic Invasion.* Contender Ministries.

2. *Interpreter's Dict. of the Bible.* 1962. Abingdon. p437.

3. *New Bible Dict..* 1962. Downers Grove IL. Intervarsity. p432.

4. Davidson, F. 1958. *The New Bible Com.* Eerdemans. p663.

5 Allen, L.C. *Word Biblical Com.* Word Books. Vol 29, p199.

6. Cook, F.C. 1897. *Holy Bible Com.* Scribner. Vol 6, p155.

7. Block, D.I. 1998. *The Book of Ezk. Ch.25-48.* Eerdemans. p435

8. Block, Op.Cit. p441.

9. Clarke, A. *The Holy Bible, A Com.* Abingdon. Vol 4, p526

10. Jensen, I.L. 1970. *Hebrews: A Self-study Guide.* Chicago. Moody Press. p6.

11. Jewett, R. 1981. *Letter to Pilgrims: A Commentary on the Epistle to the Hebrews.* N.Y. Pilgrim Press. p2

12. Attridge, H.W. 1989. *The Epistle to the Hebrews.* Phila. Fortress Press. p23.

13. Miller, W.A. 1992. *The Revelation of God to Man.* D.S.T. Thesis. Bethany Theological Seminary. p36

14. Hills, E.F. 1984. *The King James Version Defended.* Des Moines, IA. Christian Research Press. p95

15. Hughes, P.E. 1977. *A Commentary on the Epistle to the Hebrews.* Gr. Rap. MI. Eerdmans. p85

16. Rypins, S. 1951. *The Book of Thirty Centuries.* N.Y. Macmillan. p245

17. Bruce, F.F. 1970. *The English Bible.* Oxford U. Press p104

18. Evans, C.A. 2002. *The Scriptures of Jesus and His Earliest Followers.* "The Canon Debate." Ed. Mcdonald, L.M. & Sanders, J.A.

19. Strouse, T.M. Dean Burgon Society Article

20. Ellingworth, P. 1993. *Com. on Hebrews: New International Greek Testament Com.* Gr. Rapids, MI. Eerdmans. p252

21. Hagner, D.A. 1983. *Hebrews: A Good News Commentary.* San Francisco. Harper & Row. p51

22. Ellingworth. Op. Cit. p586

23. Davis, J.J. *Davis Dict. of the Bible*. Nashville. Royal. p844

24. Talmon, S. 1975. *Qumran and the History of the Biblical Text*. Ed. F.M Cross & S. Talmon. Harvard U. Press. Cambridge MA. p27

25. Strouse, T.M. 1992. *The Lord God Hath Spoken: A Guide to Bibliology*. Va. Beach. Tabernacle Baptist Theo. Press. p56.

26. Jellicoe, S. 1968. *The Septuagint and Modern Study*. Oxford at Clarendon Press. p5-18,175-188 &292

27. Bruce F.F. 1990. *The Book of Hebrews: The New Int. Com. on the New Testament*. Gr. Rap. Eerdmans. p26

28. Wurthwein, E. 1979. *The Text of the Old Testament*. Grand Rapids. Eerdmans. p26

29. *Nicene & Post-Nicene Fathers*. Christian Lit. Ed. Vol. 2. p542.

30. *New Catholic Encyclopedia*. 1967. Catholic U. of Amer. Wash. D.C. Vol. 2. p427

C. Comprehensive Refutation of Text-Evolution Theory

Unorthodox text variety

We've offered a basis for major Old-Testament text variety with the amplification concept, and now will account for much minor errata. Scholars blind to God's hand in text inerrancy, espouse textual evolution theory suggesting much variety through copyist error. They don't consider possible variety by text tampering, a viewpoint caused by devotion to Wescott and Hort theory.

A prominent evolution theory is a migrating-text notion suggesting an early consonantal (vowel-less) text in Palestine evolved into an expanded text longer than the current Masoretic.[1] Supposedly forms of this text migrated to Babylon and Alexandria, Egypt. In Babylon the text supposedly underwent abbreviation in evolution to yield a shortened text that became the basis for the Masoretic Text on migration back to Palestine. The text in Alexandria is said to have remained expanded as it evolved to yield the LXX text form. A text kept in Palestine supposedly continued evolving to yield the Samaritan Pentateuch that is actually close to the Masoretic Pentateuch. Thus the Hebrew text supposedly changed continually, and in different ways in different locales.

The Dead-Sea Scrolls were seen by many as proof of evolution. Hebrew manuscripts very close to the Masoretic Text and some with slight-moderate variance were found. Scholars see this as stages of an unsettled evolving Hebrew text. There were also texts resembling the Greek LXX or Samaritan Pentateuch in variant degree. Younger manuscripts of the 1st and 2nd centuries A.D. at Dead-Sea locales of Masada and Wadi Murabbaat are virtually identical to today's Masoretic Text. All this supposedly proves a changing early Hebrew text stabilized in the late 1st century A.D with the Babylonian-type text as the standard.

Our Lord and His disciples often quoted an LXX-type text in the New Testament, and the above view of scholars would have them endorsing an LXX Old Testament different from the autographs.

Inadequate Evolution theory: Scholars seem to think evolution of the text is unavoidable, denying divine preservation. But if evolution is so unavoidable, how does an "evolving" Pentateuch of the standard text of Jews keep close to a Samaritan-Pentateuch text evolving independently among Palestinian Samaritans so distinctly separated from the Jews. And why did an unavoidable, evolution process end in the 1st century A.D?

A. Evolution theory is a purely secular approach to text history, resulting in a notion that sacred traditional texts contain much error. Scholars endorse manuscripts showing real evidence of tampering, being fully convinced discordant manuscripts can be corrected to render them superior to harmonious traditional texts. They fully resist the concept that harmonious traditional texts are preserved providentially, and that it is wise to leave abandoned questionable ones in obscurity due to untraceable error.

B. The concept of a standard text unaltered from its inception in autographs is not disproven by Dead-Sea scrolls. Most scholars just prefer to view the evidence in terms of text evolution and standardization in the late 1st century A.D. Such interpretation is invalid, as noted recently by Schiffman [2] and earlier by Roberts [3] who found that Qumran evidence tells us the Masoretic Text-type was fully developed and predominant in Palestine in the 2nd century B.C., well before its supposed 1st century A.D. evolution culmination. This means this text-type was the standard about as far back in time as the Dead-Sea Scroll evidence takes us.

The Masoretic seems always to have been a standard from which other texts derived, as seen by the nature of the LXX, targumim and Samaritan Pentateuch. Targumim are Masoretic-Text paraphrases traceable to the 2nd century B.C.[2] The LXX is basically similar to the Masoretic and is likely a translation of an amplified Masoretic-type text, rather than a different Hebrew text, only later LXX copies being altered by corruption. And the Samaritan Pentateuch, a minor modification of a Masoretic-type text [2,4] with unorthodox variance and usually dated traditionally to the 5th-4th centuries B.C.,[2,5] is indicative of the Masoretic Text as the standard text acting as the basis for copies and translations as far back in history as the literary evidence can take us.

C. Why would one diverse manuscript group in a tiny isolated Qumran locale be part of the history of a <u>standard</u> text. It may be an aberration from an unchanging standard text. Variant forms of the Masoretic text at Qumran wouldn't likely be sent there from other locales as part of an orthodox tradition for a standard text. Was each variant form sent to, and approved by, orthodox circles in Palestine as it arose from an evolutionary process in Babylon? Or was the total collection of variant texts sent and approved as evolution was finalized? Any such history would cause textual confusion and would never spawn the common orthodox Jewish concept of an unchanging God-given standard text. It would only ensure lack of a standard text for orthodox Judaism.

As we'll see, errata in Qumran texts likely arises from the collection of distorted texts by unorthodox parties for unique uses, or from depositing of collected distorted texts discarded by orthodox parties preserving a fixed standard text.

D. The notion of evolution of different text-types in different locales isn't supported by history, as Schiffman pointed out.[2] History tells us the Hebrew text for the LXX was brought to Alexandria from Palestine, and Palestine is the one certain locale identified with the Masoretic-type and Samaritan-Pentateuch-type texts. The evidence supports a fixed text as far back in time as text history can take us, and that fixed text relates to Palestine. There is no basis to speculate about a standard-text origin by text migration from Palestine to diverse locales and back to Palestine.

E. Any assertion of evolution as the cause of Qumran manuscript diversity can be justified only by demonstrating evolution in Palestine where the texts were found. We must see the evolution process among diverse Qumran texts themselves. We must at least see a possibility of local evolution as an explanation for the diversity, but this presents a problem for scholars. Earlier they thought local evolution explained text diversity at Qumran, but they had to abandon this position due to hard facts. For example, they noted a Qumran Deuteronomy manuscript of 2nd-century B.C. vintage systematically altered from Masoretic conformity to LXX conformity, which is indicative of tampering and would be progress in the wrong direction regarding evolution toward a Masoretic-type text.[6] And there are other examples of Qumran manuscripts of published text relationships and ages [2,6,7] that defy a local evolutionary development scheme, as noted below.

1. Strongly-Masoretic Qumran manuscripts like Jeremiah A of the 3rd- century B.C, the Psalms B scroll of the 2nd-1st century B.C, Isaiah B of the 1st century B.C. and Jeremiah C of the 1st century B.C. deny an evolution process extending to the 1st century A.D. They indicate an unchanged Masoretic Text established much earlier. Jeremiah A of the 3rd century B.C. is as strongly Masoretic as Jeremiah C of the late 1st century B.C, in the heart of a supposed evolutionary period, indicating an unchanging standard Masoretic well before the late 1st century A.D.

2. The Qumran Samuel B manuscript of the late 3rd century B.C. is basically an LXX type with some lesser, but substantial, Masoretic character, while the Samuel C manuscript of the late 1st century B.C. is also an LXX type with still less Masoretic character. With these texts suggesting an LXX-type Samuel with just minor Masoretic character popular in Palestine as late as the late 1st century B.C., how can there be a fully Masoretic Samuel in Palestine by the late 1st century A.D.? An explanation based on evolution suggests an evolution process moving very slowly when it doesn't have much time left for completion before presumed finalization in the late 1st century A.D. And we might ask how it is ever going to catch up when it seems to be going in the wrong direction, Masoretic character decreasing from the 3rd to 1st centuries B.C. Can two contrasting evolution processes go on in different directions at the same time in the same locale?

3. A basically-Masoretic 2nd-century B.C. Isaiah A varies from the Masoretic more than the 1st century B.C. Isaiah B, the latter being very close to the current text. Both originated in Judea of Palestine, as did some Isaiah fragments. Some fragments are closer to B than to A regarding faithfulness to the Masoretic [6,7] and date from the early 2nd century B.C. which makes them a little older than Isaiah A. How can texts closer to the Masoretic than Isaiah A appear slightly earlier in history by local Judean evolution toward the Masoretic? Did normally slow evolution proceed backwards rapidly over less than a half century or so, then reverse itself, going forward rapidly for another half century or so. And could this occur locally in one part of Palestine over such a short time and with the consent of mainstream Judaism?

4. A late 3rd-century B.C. Jeremiah A manuscript is a strongly-Masoretic expanded text (scholars describe Masoretic Jeremiah this way), compared with Jeremiah B & D scrolls penned in the first half of the 2nd century B.C, which are shorter texts of strong LXX character. Again, an evolution process would be going in the wrong direction, from the Masoretic type toward the LXX type, and to further complicate evolution theory, Jeremiah would be reversing a normal LXX tendency toward text expansion. And dates of these texts would require evolution to occur very rapidly over about a half century when it is supposed to be a slow process. Then, from LXX Jeremiah B & D of the 2nd century B.C, we come to strongly Masoretic Jeremiah C of the 1st century B.C, and did evolution reverse direction again and also reverse its earlier text abbreviation tendency by expanding again?

Such discrepancies refute evolution theory, for an _older_ strongly Masoretic-type text can't evolve from _younger_ types of lesser Masoretic nature under any circumstances. As scholars admit, variety at Qumran can't be due to local evolution in Palestine. To justify their evolution belief, they conveniently imagine variety by evolution of isolated texts in remote locales and migration back to Palestine. This is fanciful speculation of no historic basis, that forces the evolution notion, avoids practical interpretation of the evidence and denies conscientious care of the true text by orthodox parties. If no evidence of evolution locally in or near Qumran is seen, what real basis is there to assume it occurred anywhere in Palestine, Babylon or Egypt? Regarding Qumran Isaiah manuscript types, the migrating-text theory is fully denied, for all are associated with one part of Palestine (Judea). And their ages are discordant with their degree of Masoretic conformity, so evolution toward the Masoretic Text isn't possible. Even if a text group evolved in Babylon, that group relocated in Qumran should still show evidence of evolution, but none can be found. Text variety by evolution can be justified only for Qumran where the texts were found, and the possibility of that is nil.

F. Scholars make a case for evolution mainly on the basis of perceived progression from three different text-types at Qumran to an exclusive one supposedly almost dominant in Masada manuscripts of the 1st century A.D. and fully dominant in Wadi Murabbaat manuscripts of the late 1st century A.D. But the only important difference is that between diverse Qumran texts and virtually identical ones at the other two locales. This can mean Qumran is a local aberration not at all representative of standard-text history. It's presumptuous to attach importance to texts of one isolated clannish sect living in the small isolated temporal Qumran locale. Before resorting to evolution, simpler more-likely explanations must be shown to be invalid. The ones noted earlier offer more likely, more plausible, alternatives that will now be discussed further.

Other Explanations for Text Diversity

Unorthodox diversity: Corrupt texts collected or deposited
Association of variant Qumran manuscripts with unorthodox parties is suggested in the observation of scholar Emmanuel Tov that many of them defy classification as types, being mixtures of different types to greatly different degrees.[8] Scholars say mixing

of isolated text types after migration to Palestine is a natural expected occurrence.[6] But why would mixing of variant texts of sacred literature be natural or even tolerated? Mixing would most likely result from tampering, and it's known that many Qumran manuscripts were made by Qumran residents, whose orthodoxy was very questionable, as we'll see. Mixing of text types is not consistent with orthodoxy and wouldn't arise from a natural standard-text evolution tolerated by orthodox Judaism. Such inconsistency is glaring since many diverse texts are not that far apart in time, and scholars must explain how this could happen by any natural process in orthodox circles. Orthodox parties in Palestine could see a short-term departure from text tradition in incoming foreign texts. Qumran parties likely used manuscripts available today from Qumran finds, some showing much variance over short periods of just a half century or less. Would orthodox parties accept text variance that ensured against a text tradition of their own? Qumran writers themselves claimed great orthodoxy in their alleged devotion to the exact letter of the law, and how much text diversity could they tolerate before losing knowledge of the exact letter of the law?

A. Qumran text variety is easily indicative of collection of diverse texts by local unorthodox parties for their purposes. Several texts at Qumran are very close to the current Masoretic, having virtually no differences from it, as one pro-evolution scholar expressed the matter.[7] To call them "proto-Masoretic," or changing evolutionary ancestors of the Masoretic, is speculation. They may be slightly irregular copies rejected by meticulous scribes. The perfectionist scribes of later centuries rejected copies that came close, but did not meet the high standard, and this tradition likely originated much earlier. Rejected copies might well be the best available to Essene Qumran residents since they were a fringe sect hostile to the temple priesthood and would not have access to standard temple manuscripts. Qumran Masoretic-type texts of mild variance may be slightly imperfect rejected copies.

And Masoretic-type manuscripts of pronounced variance present a possibility of corruption in duplication by incompetent scribes, or manipulation by dishonest ones. Before any evolution theory is proposed, we need to know if Qumran writers were poor copyists or how text manipulation might serve their interests.

We also need to know how far any interest in text diversity extended. Qumran LXX and Samaritan-Pentateuch type texts are sharply differentiated from the Masoretic type. The former were few in number compared with the Masoretic, indicating limited availability by contrast with general availability of a standard orthodox Masoretic Text from the outside world. Emmanuel Tov noted that Qumran Masoretic-type manuscripts are closer to the current Masoretic Text than other types are to their LXX and Samaritan-Pentateuch relatives.[9] Perhaps these latter text types were more poorly preserved as a consequence of a non-standard textual basis not so well established as a standard Masoretic Text.

The writers' involvement in diversity extended to extremes in their appetite for non-canonical apocrypha comprising a large portion of the literary cache there, a subject we'll address shortly.

B. Another plausible reason for Qumran text variety is that the texts are the contents of a repository for unorthodox biblical-type materials collected by orthodox parties in Palestine and disposed of by burying in caves. The concept is like that of the synagogue geniza for storing old bible manuscripts to prevent desecration. In this case a desert location would likely be chosen in lieu of a synagogue since the texts would be seen as unorthodox, yet requiring respect since they contained some scripture. Gathering of diverse texts from some locales might arise as Jerusalem elders examined variant texts causing confusion, and the likely result would be disposal with respect. This would be initiated by the pharisaic/rabbinic movement in its historic effort to eliminate undesirable texts (including apocrypha) that would culminate in the 1st century A.D. after the movement became predominant.

Variant texts arise due to a persistent tendency of scholars to have scripture conform to their views of text history and teaching. This problem marks modern versions produced by any scholar who feels qualified, and such versions experience corruption, eventual obscurity or confinement to unbiblical groups. For the welfare of bible-believers, there must be a way to handle confusion caused by those who appoint themselves to render God's Word without His calling. Obsolescence corruption discussed earlier serves this way, unauthorized work being evident in a few decades usually, though this may change as the present apostasy advances, with scholars promoting, rather than rejecting, corrupt texts.

C. Another non-evolutionary repository-type explanation for Qumran-text diversity is proposed by a notable scholar.[10] He has postulated that many manuscripts were deposited at Qumran and Masada by Jerusalem residents for safe-keeping during the 1st-century A.D. melee just prior to the Roman conquest of the city. By this theory, manuscripts of both locales would support the concept of a standard Masoretic Text in Judaism, challenged by variant texts, rather than that of an evolving text. Jerusalem would be the source of <u>competing</u> standard and non-standard Hebrew texts utilized <u>together in history</u> in the center of orthodoxy. The orthodox texts could belong to orthodox parties, and others to sectarian rebels. The theory proposes orthodox texts kept in the care of the orthodox Masada residents, and the unorthodox texts cached at Qumran. This would indicate sectarianism in Jerusalem competing with orthodoxy, and acceptance of apocrypha within Judaism shortly before its elimination by the rabbinic movement, such literature being emphasized by sectarians for their purposes.

Before scholars can say the mere presence of text variety at a tiny Qumran settlement supports the notion of an evolving text of all Judaism, they must show that more likely explanations don't apply. They must prove that Qumran literature wasn't unorthodox debris, and did represent an uncertain text state common to all

Judaic society. Indeed the burden of proof is entirely on scholars when they assume such an unlikely thing for orthodox Judaism.

These alternative explanations account for extreme variety at Qumran that includes variant text-type, content, language (Hebrew, Aramaic, Greek), script type and highly variant spelling convention.[9] Why would orthodox Judaism accumulate such text variety? To assume evolution as the cause of variety is highly unwarranted when simpler and more likely causes apply.

Unorthodox Diversity:
Corruption by Qumran Writers

Theory on an unsettled highly-variant scripture text should make us ask why Qumran writers would have an unlikely confused text. How can scholars conclude that a great text variety would suit a group they say were, according to their self-descriptive literature, devoted to a meticulous adherence to the letter of the law? How could they be so in the absence of a fixed text of the law? Even if Qumran texts had only local use in the community, such text variety would be most unlikely for any orthodox group in recorded history, especially within Palestinian Judaism. We must ask how representative of orthodox Judaism and its literary diet Qumran writers and their manuscripts really were.

Qumran text manipulation: Motives and evidence

Unique motives of Qumran residents (or whoever deposited the texts) are indicated in that many manuscripts in their cache are of a content and language/spelling style that suggests modification of the Masoretic-type text.[2] Perhaps the writers sought many biblical texts in support of their interpretations of doctrine, and on not finding what they sought, modified the respected standard text. This can explain many moderately-variant Masoretic-type texts at Qumran, and would not be surprising in the Essene sect known to have rebelled in hatred against the priesthood at Jerusalem where scripture seems always to have been revered.

In exploring Qumran literature, we must study evidence on the writers' view of the canon. Scholars say their texts indicate the Hebrew canon wasn't finalized at this time. The Book of Esther, and possibly Nehemiah [11] weren't used, and certain apocryphal books were used with the authority of scripture. And scholars say use at Qumran of Psalms texts that were a mixture of canonical Psalms and Apocrypha, suggests an unfinalized canon at that time in history. They seem to think apocrypha would be accepted as scripture if it were not for men's opinions, despite the fact it's so clearly inferior to canonical books.

But how can they conclude that Qumran proves Esther was not yet a canonical book and that the Psalms content was not yet finalized this late in history? How can scholars know the Qumran writers stayed strictly with texts accepted among the orthodox? How can they know the writers had a typical Hebrew reverence for the canonical text? Their failure to acknowledge the book of Esther can reflect self-serving selective use of a settled canon. Esther had political significance for the Hasmoneans [12] known to be hated by the Essenes, and hatred could take precedence over devotion to scripture. Qumran literature reveals knowedge of the book,[2] so the writers ignored a book in the standard text, perhaps because they were Essenes who hated the Hasmoneans.

And authoritative use of Psalms mixed with apocryphal passages by the writers may have no bearing whatever on the state of the canon. They may simply have exalted apocrypha due to its nationalistic importance and their extreme nationalism (as with the Essenes), or due to its support of their unique doctrine. In this regard, despite adopting much apocrypha, the writers never refer to 1st Maccabees a primary apocryphal nationalistic book emphasizing Hasmonaen history. Perhaps hatred for the Hasmonaens exceeded their own nationalist fervor, a fervor that otherwise would promote 1st Maccabees.

Qumran writers didn't have the traditional Hebrew regard for supreme authority of scripture, as indicated in their misuse of it in commentaries. They misquoted or changed texts to support their beliefs.[13] Another troubling tendency was a lack of restraint in using scripture to justify matters having a superficial relationship to scripture teaching.[13] Thus they may have mixed Psalms with apocrypha for self-serving ends. Qumran writers likely did not respect the sanctity of scripture, in contrast with the much larger Pharisee and Sadducee sects of Judaism. The Pharisees did invent laws they added to the biblical base, but never said they were of divine origin, considering them as a "fence around the law" meant to ensure the law itself wasn't violated (Their indictment by Christ was for adding private-interpretation burdens to scripture, something characteristic of the Qumran writers). The Pharisees had private interpretations, but didn't change scripture, the matter in which Qumran writers seem notably unorthodox.

Devotion to God's truth is found among those of Judaism who regarded scripture from the most orthodox viewpoint. Among these, history reveals measures for preservation of God's Word that were hardly short of martyrdom, and this is where assurance of the identity of the true text is best sought. This source gave us our Masoretic Text of today, and in this tradition one finds the highest possible fidelity to accurate transmission of scripture.

On the other hand, at Qumran one finds evidence of carelessness or manipulation in manuscript copying,[14,15,16] not surprising in a small isolated sect that might use scripture for its own purposes. Predominance of a standard Masoretic Text, unsupportive of sect unique doctrines, could lead to modifying it to produce, in a respected biblical base, harmony with their doctrines. Indeed the Isaiah A scroll, one of the oldest, at Qumran, and clearly in the Masoretic tradition overall, shows signs of carelessness and manipulation of the text.[14,15,16] It's informative to note that Isaiah A, with its evident text changes, is part of the portion of Qumran literature directly copied by the Qumran writers. Evidence of self-serving manipulation is indicated in recent studies showing the text of Isaiah A was changed at Isaiah 8:11 at Qumran to justify supposed fulfillment of scriptural prophecy by Qumran residents.[14] Such notions preoccupied Qumran writers, judging by their commentaries,[13] and it's little wonder Isaiah was popular at Qumran. Furthermore, some Qumran scrolls show evidence of additions to the Pentateuch, and, as noted, likely combining of canonical Psalms and apocrypha. Such findings are indicative of inadequate respect for the Judaic standard that makes scripture, God's Word, the supreme authority.

Thus the Qumran Isaiah A isn't likely what scholars suggest, part of an unstable evolving Hebrew text that had achieved major, but incomplete, Masoretic form in a developing standardization that would later exclude other text types. More likely, it illustrates corruption of a fixed text by copyists serving interests of a sect.

Qumran: A theological Aberration
The likelihood that Qumran-writer mentality was conducive to altering scripture becomes evident upon considering the cultic nature of their theology. They were a break-away sect with some views well removed from the rigid ones of orthodox Judaism. As already discussed, they appear to be most shaky at the very point where Judaism as a whole was inalterably orthodox, namely the inviolable nature of scripture that transcends all private opinion.

The sect that deposited the manuscripts are most commonly thought by scholars to be the small Essene Judaic group residing at Qumran (various other sects residing there and elsewhere have been suggested). The sect's self-descriptive literature reveals a superiority mentality. They were monastic ascetic exclusivists requiring unique initiation rites, oaths and probationary periods of examination for membership. They were marked by a conviction that they alone could enter heaven, and were inclined to keep secretive among themselves knowledge they considered essential to righteousness and salvation. They seem to have been devoted to observance of Mosaic law, but only according to their private interpretation. As suggested, extreme devotion to their nationalist understanding of the Old Testament may have been a cause of eventual loss of their sense of the inviolable nature of scripture.

And they were hostile to others in Judaic society. They were sympathetic to an old Zadokite Sadducean priesthood that they considered orthodox and hated the Hasmonaean priesthood that usurped authority after Maccabean Wars. They hated Pharisees whom they saw as compromisers, despite the Pharisees' fame for legalism and their lack of favor with the Hasmoneans.

In summary, Qumran-sect character was marked by cultic practices extraneous to mainstream orthodox Judaism, including inadequate respect for scripture, extreme hatred for many of their peers and their unique type of practice of exclusivity.

Qumran: An appetite for unorthodox literature

That a standard Masoretic Text was altered by the Qumran sect, or outsiders, is indicated by the variety of texts found there. Apocrypha and pseudepigrapha constituted a third of the total literary cache. As noted, the residents even seem to have equated authority of such literature with that of canonical texts.[17] Pseudepigrapha (tales falsely attributed to the Old Testament patriarchs) and apocrypha (hidden things) "expand" or paraphrase scripture, adding material not in canonical books. Well-known apocryphal books of Enoch and Jubilees evidently were revered by Qumran residents. Other apocryphal books in use included Testaments of Naphtali, Levi and Kohath, a Genesis paraphrase and Tobit.[18] Great esteem of Qumran residents for the Jubilees book is seen by their adoption of a unique calendar linked to the book.[17] The book is quoted by them with authority reserved for scripture by Jews, despite its non-canonical status. This is most ominous in view of the book's own claims to be divine revelation.

Of special note is discovery at Qumran of texts of a Book of Giants of known association with the Persian mystical religion, Manicheism[18] that springs largely from ancient dualism of the Persian Zoroastrian religion. Zoroastrianism appears to have had much influence on ancient dualistic Gnosticism that plagued the early church. Dualism divided the world into two inalterable good and evil forces in constant inevitable conflict with each other, but not competing for adherents, a number being assigned to each one by fate. The material human body was considered inherently evil, but could be redeemed by knowledge given by exclusive revelation to a privileged class. These tenets of Dualism are comparable to basic notions of Gnosticism (and Essenism) found in the Qumran sect that, like Gnosticism and Manicheism, may have been influenced by Zorastrianism. In the sect's "Rule of the Community" is seen the Dualistic/Gnostic doctrine of two dominating opposing good and evil world forces beyond the power of men. The fatalism might be tempered by God, but contrasts with scripture teaching of God offering hope to all, and man beset with original disabling sin in his pursuit of righteousness. Dualistic/Gnostic aspects of the sect's doctrine are seen in their conviction that they were sole possessors of special divine revelation that redeemed the soul, and also in their low valuation of the body reflected in their asceticism.

Dualism evidently appealed to those who felt superior in knowledge of the sublime. It's no surprise that apocrypha, that could be viewed as special revelation for the elite, was popular at elitist Qumran. And the LXX and Samaritan-Pentateuch biblical texts might seem to elitist Qumran residents as revelation meant providentially for their privileged estate. It's also no surprise that literature about the occult, like astrology and magic was fairly popular at Qumran, as this too might suggest unique revelation for the sect. Or extreme nationalism might lead the sect to adopt even the obvious error of their nation rejected by the orthodox.

To suggest Qumran texts reflect standard-text history is foolish. They're likely an aberration from that history offering no support at all for evolution theory. We get a far more useful view of text history from Hebrew orthodoxy in relation to text amplification.

A Divinely Preserved Fixed Orthodox Text

Evolution theory on text variety is far from consistent enough with logic and fact to obligate us to accept it for truth's sake. It's just one interpretation of the evidence, and there's far too much suggestion of corruption by unorthodox or incompetent scribes, or text collector/repository activity. We consider ways in which manuscript evidence speaks of the history of a fixed standard text faithful to inerrant autographs, but partly obscured by variety in Qumran scrolls and other ancient texts.

More details on orthodox text history
A text history affirming a continuing fixed Masoretic-type text isn't difficult to envision from the evidence. It begins with highly faithful transmission of the Masoretic Text among Jews known throughout the last millennium of the Christian era, which can be a latter stage of a continuing ancient text tradition. 1st-2nd century A.D. strongly Masoretic-type texts from Wadi Murabbaat and Masada locales would reflect an unchanged standard Hebrew-text tradition derived from very ancient originals. Scholars consider variant texts at Qumran as representing an earlier scripture diet of all Judaism since there is little older evidence by which to identify the standard. But age isn't a conclusive factor since there is great danger of aberration from text history at this one small isolated locale. Likely, at the Wadi Murabbaat site located ~11 miles from Qumran, fully Masoretic manuscripts found there represent an ancient standard text we happen to view at a given time in the 2nd century A.D, later than we view Qumran texts. These scrolls may differ from Qumran texts because they were the property of Jews who preserved an ancient standard, those of the pharisaic/rabbinic tradition dominant at this time.

And strongly Masoretic-type biblical manuscripts of the 1st-century A.D. found at Masada may be another view of a standard Masoretic-type text we happen to see at a certain point in time. These belonged to more orthodox Jews of the Pharisaic/rabbinic movement, and varied slightly from today's Masoretic. They included a little apocryphal material, but this may be just a matter of variable chronology in our view of the effort by the movement to eliminate non-standard texts. Elimination of unorthodox texts, to avoid any confusion over the identity of the standard text was evidently achieved. Scholars suggest the movement promoted its favorite among evolved text-types, but more likely it preserved an older recognized standard text by eliminating unorthodox rivals. This would include apocrypha prevalent earlier at Qumran and potentially very troublesome for maintenance of the standard.

Scholars can't assume that Qumran, Masada and Wadi-Murabaat texts represent three evolution stages ending in the late 1st century. They can be three different chronological views of the state of the standard text during the Pharisaic/rabbinic movement's effort to eliminate non-standard texts. The effort, climaxing in the late 1st century, wouldn't have developed earlier at Qumran, allowing for substantial variance and much apocryphal material in an isolated fringe group. By the time of Masada, the effort would be close to finalization, resulting in a little retained non-standard material. Wadi Murabaat texts, observed a little later than Masada texts, would represent full triumph of the effort to restore predominance of the Masoretic Text and eliminate non-standard texts, rather than a culmination of evolution.

LXX Amplification: A Conclusion of Orthodox Diversity

Amplification or evolution in LXX text history?
We continue discussion of amplification with final details on the LXX role. The aim here is to show that nuances of LXX text history provide a fit with the amplification/obsolescence concept and further support an orthodox alternative to evolution.

Corruption in the Greek LXX included later efforts to modify it to better agreement with the Masoretic standard. Amplification was likely removed by revisers, including Jews who wanted to distinguish the LXX from the text of Christians later in text history. Such modification is known in LXX revisions toward the Masoretic in the early-church era, due to conflict between Jews and Christians over LXX wording regarding Christology.

But scholars think there were periodic earlier B.C. revisions of the LXX to keep pace with a supposedly-evolving standard Hebrew text of Palestine. Supposedly, LXX revision followed evolutionary change in a standard Hebrew text[7]presumed to have been changing by abbreviation of a fuller Palestinian text. It is presumed the LXX text-form called "expanded" Lucianic was the result of a B.C. revision of a more original LXX, the revision supposedly being made to follow changes in an early evolving proto-Masoretic Palestinian Hebrew text that was shrinking, but still expanded. This evolving Hebrew text is supposedly reflected in a manuscript like the 1st century B.C. Samuel A at Qumran that is a mixed Hebrew text with basic Lucianic LXX character. Then later, at a date estimated to range from the late 1st century B.C. to the second half of the 1st century A.D., the Lucianic-type LXX text was supposedly revised toward a Hebrew text current in Palestine at that time that had evolved still closer to the final Masoretic, producing what scholars call the Kaige LXX revision. Supposedly, by the late 1st century A.D, Hebrew text evolution ended in strongly-Masoretic Jewish revisions of the Kaige text produced in the 2nd-3rd centuries A.D. to counteract the Christian LXX. These latter, three in number, are known after their authors as the Aquila, Theodotion and Symmachus texts.

This is just speculation based on the assumption that evolution explains the evidence. Kaige is the crucial kingpin in the theory of a series of evolving Hebrew texts, and there is no known Hebrew text that could serve as a basis for Kaige, even among the wide variety of Hebrew texts at Qumran. Thus there is no known series of Hebrew texts and no known evolution path the Greek texts could follow. The so-called series of Greek texts can't be called a series, but texts that only conform to the Masoretic Text in variant degree. And the Aquila, Theodotion and Symmachus Masoretic-like Greek texts, supposedly the termination of a B.C./A.D evolution process, are historically known to be due to disputes of Jews and Christians, limited to an A.D. time frame.

The notion of LXX revisions following an evolving Hebrew text is further refuted in that Symmachus and Aquila, and possibly Theodotion, may not be revisions, but new translations of the Hebrew text. This is what ancient witnesses tell us,[19] and latest scholarship indicates Aquila and Symmachus were new translations of the Hebrew, not LXX revisions.[19] Thus the translators, rather than following an evolving Hebrew text, likely sought greater Masoretic conformity in a Greek translation for Jews

Then we address the scholar notion that Symmachus and Aquila Greek texts were made using the Kaige LXX revision with its partial Masoretic conformity as a starting basis and the full Masoretic for final correction.[6] This is contradicted by historic testimony and latest scholarship which, as noted, indicate both versions were made by translating from a fully Masoretic Hebrew text. Thus scholars can't distinguish between an LXX-styled text corrected in one step to the standard Masoretic and an LXX text corrected in two steps, first to an "evolved" partly Masoretic Kaige-type, then to a fully Masoretic Hebrew text. The "evolving" partially-Masoretic Hebrew text for Kaige that scholars postulate looks like a mere figment of their imagination.

An Orthodox View of LXX Text History:

Non-evolutionary relationships among historic LXX texts
The amplified Hebrew text proposed by this writer, appearing late in the history of a progressively-revealed standard text, would underlie an orthodox Lucianic LXX. Kaige can be a text-type arising from a later partial adaptation of the Lucianic to a fixed standard Masoretic Text for reasons noted below.

Before the church era, the LXX was highly regarded by Jews, and the desire to modify it would be due to embarrassment over seeming text corruption suggested by comparing its amplified text with the Masoretic standard. This could happen among both Hellenist Jews in Egypt comparing the LXX with the Masoretic, and among Palestinian Jews comparing the amplified Hebrew manuscripts for the LXX with the Masoretic. Many such Jews could lose touch with knowledge of an orthodox origin of the LXX text in an orthodox amplified Hebrew text. This situation offers an orthodox explanation for nuances of LXX text history that scholars interpret as evidence of evolution.

The alternative begins with the assertion that there was no Hebrew-text evolution. Rather, an original Lucianic-type LXX would be the original LXX with expansion by providential amplification present from the beginning by transference from its amplified Hebrew original. And the manuscripts related to the Samuel A would contain the amplified Hebrew text from which the original Lucianic LXX was translated. Further changes by later obsolescence corruption would alter amplification in the LXX and its Hebrew-text basis throughout.

Regarding Kaige, it may be a modification of the Lucianic LXX, but this doesn't prove revision by correction to a proto-Masoretic evolving text. As noted, the theory that kaige was a further revision of the Lucianic text toward a Hebrew text that had evolved closer to the current Masoretic isn't substantiated by evidence. No Hebrew text associated with Kaige has been found at Qumran (or elsewhere), despite the fact that text variety was so notable there. Evidence that the Kaige LXX revision was actually patterned after a text fully in Masoretic form, rather than an evolving proto-Masoretic text, is seen in the work of K.G. O' Connell.[20] He found that Kaige in Exodus is the result of revision of the LXX toward the standard Masoretic text, suggesting this text was the standard before the late 1st-century B.C./A.D. Kaige origin. He assumed a proto-Masoretic Hebrew text fully evolved in Exodus and not in other books, but until a Hebrew text of such mixture is found, this is speculation. If it did exist, its authenticity would have to be proven objectively rather than by associating it with an imagined evolutionary scheme, as scholars would likely do. If we know the standard Masoretic was used for any book of Kaige, it is more logical to assume the standard text was in use at that time in history, than to imagine an evolving proto-Masoretic to account for books not fully reflecting Masoretic modification. Why would random evolution be so precise as to finalize in one book? There's a more likely orthodox reason for variance from full conformity to the Masoretic Text among Kaige books.

A non-evolving Hebrew text accounts for Kaige deviation from the standard Masoretic in some books, in the realization that the LXX and its amplified Hebrew text were highly revered by Jews, hindering modification at first. This explains Kaige as a partial modification toward a standard Masoretic text restrained by the Jews' reverence for scripture, not modification to an evolving Masoretic Text. Jewish restraint could be due to uncertainty on how to handle two revered texts and puzzlement about whether the amplified text should be retained in places. The result might well be limited Masoretic adaptation in places where this was deemed essential, and retention of the amplified text elsewhere. Restraint would be much encouraged by published testimony supportive of the LXX in a famous Letter of Aristeas. Supportive testimony was perpetuated for centuries in writings of the Jewish notables, Philo the philosopher and Josephus the historian.

It is not difficult to envision how restrained Kaige-type revision of the LXX could occur. The amplified text likely was known by some in Jerusalem in books like Chronicles through the auspices of Ezra, the traditional author of Chronicles closely associated with rebuilding of Jerusalem after Babylonian Captivity. Ezra is also the one likely associated with advanced amplification in a Hebrew text for the later LXX. As noted, this latter association of Ezra is indicated in that the Chronicles by Ezra are uniquely similar to Lucianic LXX renderings in a Hebrew LXX-type manuscript like Samuel A. The amplification concept would be verified at Jerusalem by Ezra and associates. Jerusalem elders would view the amplified Hebrew text for the LXX the same way Christians viewed the New Testament, the latest progressive unveiling of new parts of the standard text, clarifying elements of the history and future of God's people. And the Pentateuch of the

LXX would be seen as a providentially-advanced state of the type of amplification that Deuteronomy provides on other earlier books of the law.

Thus the Aristeus letter-writer and Philo would be correct to say the original Pentateuch text for the LXX came from Jerusalem with full approval of Jewish authority. They would be correct to say the LXX Pentateuch translation was by elders/scholars authorized by the high priest. A company like this would be vital to show the latest providential revelation was backed by Jewish authority. This would be very necessary to ensure acceptance of Old Testament books of more highly amplified nature to be brought to Alexandria later for translation into Greek.

Well after Pentateuch translation, Alexandrian Jews would lose touch with an orthodox Hebrew basis of the LXX, and begin challenging differences from the standard text. Thus scholars would be correct in saying the Aristeus letter was a defense of the LXX meant to defeat efforts to revise it and bring it closer to the standard ext. Indeed their dating of the letter to the 2nd half of the 2nd century B.C., allows time for many Jews to lose touch with an original Jerusalem approval of the amplified Hebrew text, about 100-150 years after 3rd century B.C. translation of the LXX Pentateuch. While the Aristeas letter purports to be an account of the 3rd-century B.C. LXX project, it may just recount a later writer's understanding of the account of the real Aristeas.

A contest between LXX defenders and revisers would arise due to two different perspectives. LXX defenders would be those who retained an appreciation of its authenticity from inexact tradition. Revisers would be those in later generations who had lost touch with Jerusalem authentication of the LXX amplified text and assumed corruption had occurred and assumed a need to bring it into better conformity with a revered standard-type text far more ancient than the 3rd-2nd century B.C. LXX (indicating the Masoretic is truly ancient). Reviser's views could easily be increasingly rigid as later increasingly-amplified LXX books

102

appeared in 2nd-century B.C. Alexandria. Their reactions would be ordained as part of an obsolescence process removing the interim amplified text from its authoritative status eventually.

The Aristeas letter-writer, and later Philo, offered vigorous defenses of the LXX, and the two likely did embellish the truth to enhance their arguments. Philo would be correct in alleging a prophetic authority to the LXX, but wrong in ascribing it to the translators, this quality being in the underlying Hebrew text. In accord with the historical record, Aristeas may have been correct to ascribe excellent translation of the Hebrew by the translators, this being obscured in later copies due to obsolescence. Aristeus and Philo, writing as much as 150 and 250 years after the LXX Pentateuch origination, wouldn't likely understand all details of its history and Hebrew-text basis. Likely, the Greek LXX very early became the acclaimed latest source of revelation, while its Hebrew parent text remained in the shadows, as we expect of a people who would prefer their language in a Ptolemaic Greek-speaking part of Egypt. A popular inaccuracy over the source of revelation would continue with Josephus who wrote around 350 years after LXX Pentateuch origination. We should not expect the three men to have accurate understanding of the text history, and any error or disagreement that can be seen isn't surprising.

Thus, following in the train of the Lucianic LXX and Kaige versions, the texts of Aquila, Theodotion and Symmachus, would not be indicative of modification of the Greek to a fully-evolved Masoretic text. They would be modification efforts unrestrained now due to vehement reaction of Jews to what seemed to them to be misuse of the LXX to promote Christianity. But even in view of the heated debates of the church era, it is likely that Jews would be very reluctant to modify the LXX text if they revered it as sacred scripture. That they did revere it thusly would be indicated if we knew the translators of the three Jewish versions were Gentile proselytes to Judaism lacking traditional reverence of Jews toward scripture. Indeed many scholars think the Aquila and Theodotion texts, were made by Gentile proselytes, and there are indications the Symmachus text was also. The Kaige translator is unidentified, but if his work originated in the 1st century B.C., as scholars propose, a Jewish proselyte would be the likely one to undertake the dreaded task. If all four texts were the work of proselytes, evidence for Jewish reverence of the LXX would be very strong, as this would totally eliminate native Jewish involvement in a dreaded task. Perhaps lack of knowledge of the identity of the Kaige translator reflects his need to remain anonymous about a task dreaded at this time in history.

But the discoverer of Kaige assigned its beginning to the second half of the 1st century A.D., which also would indicate Kaige is not a product of evolution. Kaige may be the first and thus most restrained of Jewish reactions to Christian use of the LXX. Its incomplete standard-text compliance could be due to an origin early enough for Jewish modification efforts on a revered text to be restrained compared with those of the later Aquila, Theodotion and Symmachus texts. Earnest LXX modification by acknowledged translators likely would occur only after heated interchange with Christians diminished Jewish restraint.

Among those with an orthodox attitude toward scripture, restraint in modifying a revered text makes much more sense than acceptance and promotion of an "evolving" text. Regarding O' Connell's work, we note that full modification of Exodus in Kaige toward the standard text would be less likely to violate an attitude of Jewish restraint since Masoretic/LXX differences are milder in the Pentateuch than elsewhere. This may be due to original minimal departure of the LXX from the standard text in the Pentateuch where need for amplification would be minimal. Or it may be due to a less restrained imposed LXX conformity to the Masoretic-type text in the Pentateuch where the Masoretic Text would be seen as the ultimate standard of the law.

Identity of an Original LXX Text

LXX history suggests that the known Lucianic text represents an original LXX with original differences from the Masoretic due to amplification, rather than a tracking of Hebrew-text evolution.

A Cairo Deuteronomy papyrus fragment, Faoud 266, penned around 100 B.C. is said by the scholar Vaccari to be a specimen of a more reliable earlier LXX-type text superior to 4th- century A.D. Vaticanus.[21] Faoud 266 superiority is evident in that, while the text is akin to Vaticanus in general, it doesn't have obvious corruptions found in no manuscript but Vaticanus. The earlier Faoud 266 may take us back beyond the LXX corruption process in Vaticanus. Faoud 266 may represent an early 2nd-century B.C. text resistant to aligning an original (amplified) LXX with the Masoretic in the alteration process that the Letter of Aristeus contended against. As such it would be significantly closer to the original LXX than Vaticanus following in its train much later.

We may be taken still further beyond corruption processes of Vaticanus by the still-earlier Manchester Greek Papyrus 458 of 150 B.C. or earlier vintage. This is from a Greek Bible even more different from the current LXX-type text and perhaps close to an original LXX. This papyrus has been declared by Vaccari as an early form of the Lucianic LXX,[21] the original of which the present writer proposes was the original LXX. This manuscript may be close to the early LXX that Philo and the Aristeus Letter writer defended against revisers, the chronology according to scholar dating being right for such considerations.

More about the Lucianic text

The scholarly Christian martyr Lucian worked at Antioch on LXX revision, at or near the beginning of the 4th century A.D.[21] Lucian seems to have had recourse to a very early Old Greek text, one in use ~500 years or more before his time, judging by the age of the Manchester papyrus. A text of an age that takes us back beyond a demonstrably corrupt LXX text prevailing after major early-church LXX modifications, even beyond 1st-century B.C./A.D. Kaige, likely is very relevant in clarifying the identity of the original LXX, yet won't take us all the way back to the original. But Lucian and others may have recognized an ancient

LXX text-type preferred to increasingly corrupt LXX texts of their day and suitable for LXX restoration. The authenticity of Lucian's type of text is seen in its popularity in the early church.

The Lucianic-type text, not the Vaticanus, seems to be the authoritative Old Testament of the early church. Lucian's text-type was well recognized and very popular in early centuries of the church and for centuries more in some churches. It appears in earliest major bible versions of eastern and western churches in the 2nd century A.D. and later.[22,23,24] Included very early were the Old Latin, Armenian, Sahidic Coptic and elements of the Syriac Peshitta, followed after Lucian's time by the Syro-Lucianic, Gothic and Slavonic. It was well recognized and quoted by early western and eastern church notables,[22,24] including Tertullian, Cyprian, Hippolytus, Theophilus of Antioch, Clement of Alexandria, Origen, Philo and Josephus, and among later ones, Jacob of Edessa, Theodore of Mopsuestia, Augustine, Ambrose, Lucifer, Eustathius, Diodore of Tarse and Asterius Sophista. The Kaige anonymous penman of the 1st century B.C./A.D. recognized Lucianic text popularity in a different way, using it as his basis in modifying a text to bring it closer to the Masoretic, judging by studies in Samuel and Kings.[6] Theodotion in the 2nd century A.D, may have continued this recognition, bringing this adjusted-Lucianic Kaige text even closer to the Masoretic to counteract Christian use of the LXX (scholars see a relation of Theodotion to Kaige). Justyn Martyr evidently recognized an adjusted-Lucianic Kaige.[20,21] Such observations indicate ancients of the beginning of the early church, and centuries after, recognized a true old Lucianic-type LXX text, one from which the text later departed greatly in a manuscript like Vaticanus. Lack of such status for Vaticanus, despite preference for this text-type by Origen and Jerome, is seen in that Vaticanus was abandoned by churches shortly after its 4th-century A.D. origination.

Early Lucianic-LXX authenticity becomes compelling when we learn that New Testament quotes of the Old, that should preserve original LXX readings, reflect the present Lucianic LXX better than the present Vaticanus, corruption in both notwithstanding.[25] And in Samuel the Lucianic text is closer than the Vaticanus to the text of the amplified Masoretic Chronicles.[6] The original Lucianic text can be the amplified LXX quoted in the New Testament and related to amplified Masoretic Chronicles. Efforts to modify Vaticanus textual ancestors toward the Masoretic would be one way it was distanced from the New Testament quotes of the Old and from Chronicles, removal of providential amplification producing shortened readings.

Summary of Postulated Non-Evolutionary LXX Text History
To summarize the matter of LXX corruption, the identity of the original LXX is decisively declared in that, even in its present corrupt form, the Lucianic is closer than the corrupt Vaticanus to Old Testament quotations in the New Testament, so the present Lucianic is closer to the original LXX. Further clarification is provided in the affinity of the amplified Masoretic Chronicles with the amplified Lucianic Samuel text. It seems Providence has given a text association in the amplification sequence, showing us Lucianic-LXX authenticity through the combined canonical authority of the New Testament and Masoretic Chronicles. This postulated view of the LXX record suggests a visible record of an original Lucianic text, beginning with the Manchester 458 papyrus of the mid-2nd century B.C, descended from an original Lucianic LXX. The Aristeus letter writer in the second half of the 2nd century B.C. would defend this LXX type against revision, resistance to revision being represented by a late 2nd- early 1st century B.C. manuscript like Faoud 266. The revision would culminate in the 4th century A.D. Vaticanus that, in addition to shortening, sustained other indiscriminate errors.

Well after a 3rd- century B.C. LXX Pentateuch origin, Alexandrian Hellenist Jews could easily lose touch with knowledge of the true origin of the Lucianic LXX in amplified Palestinian Hebrew manuscripts. But Philo shows the tenacity of Lucianic-

LXX tradition among some Hellenist Jews in his spirited defense of it ~250 years after the initial 3rd - century B.C. Pentateuch origination. And the early church declares the Lucianic-type text as its true LXX Old Testament, as shown by the great popularity of this text in early centuries and in the east in later centuries and by rejection of Vaticanus not long after it was penned. Jewish modifications of the Greek Bible would signify decreasingly restrained efforts to assert Masoretic conformity in accord with the providential obsolescence plan to ensure the Masoretic as the standard. The Masoretic Text preserved within itself earlier major and minor amplification elements, and the New Testament preserved some advanced LXX amplification.

The hand of Providence appears, the Greek Christological LXX being a forerunner of New Testament revelation soon to spread to Greek-speaking Christians in the geographical areas of Greek-speaking Hebrews for whom the LXX was made. We consider the figure Providence made central to understanding events in LXX text history for the church, the maligned martyr Lucian. While little is known of him, he is said to have been a champion of literal scripture interpretation and a strong adversary of allegory. But he's also said to have held unorthodox views on the full deity of Christ. Yet the eastern church seems never to have taken much action against him. He was expelled from the church for a time, but later welcomed back, making us wonder about accuracy of the charges. Despite scholar negative evaluations of him, suggesting less than perfect devotion to Christ,[26] his martyrdom proves his final perfect devotion. As the record of history speaks of Lucian, it says his contemporaries held him in the highest esteem regarding scholarship and Christian integrity.[24] Not all agreed with Lucian on the direction of his scholarship, but that is no criterion by which to judge his work, for truth is often shunned by multitudes in favor of bias. Lucian wasn't just a great scholar but, unlike modern scholars, he was a man of great faith, sealing his commitment to Christ at the cost of his life. We should ask which modern scholar has that kind of commitment to Christ and thus has that kind of credibility.

Josephus on original LXX text identity and amplification
The truth of original LXX-text identity is best sought among conservative writers chronologically much closer to a knowledge of the truth than modern scholars. Josephus, writing in the 1st century A.D, has far more credibility than they, and he denies evolution in saying the Old Testament had from antiquity been kept by the Jews in sacred trust undefiled by men's errors.[27] This author is more authoritative than scholars as much as 1900 years further removed from certainty of knowledge on this subject.

But we may doubt this observation if Josephus doesn't show evidence of the standard text in his scripture quotes. Scholars find it difficult to classify his text due to his paraphrasing and because they believe his text was mixed. It's thought he used both a Hebrew text (It has been called simply Semitic) and a Lucianic LXX, the latter from 1 Samuel onward.[21,24] Josephus includes the Lucianic LXX with a Hebrew-type text in speaking of an unchanged Old Testament, which fits the concept of an amplified LXX once recognized by orthodox Jews as a providential advance in the standard text. The fit is seen by Josephus' adoption of the amplified text beginning in 1 Samuel, which isn't likely capricious, for the Masoretic 1 Samuel links to identifiable amplification in the Masoretic Chronicles and thus in the Lucianic LXX (noted, p106). Josephus evidently saw the link of amplification to Samuel, accepting Lucianic LXX amplification of Samuel as part of unveiling of the standard text, believing the best understanding of 1 Samuel would be found in the amplified Lucianic LXX text.

Josephus made his comments in 93-94 A.D. at a time when a Masoretic-type text is said by scholars to have stopped evolving and become the standard." This Jewish historian, writing at the end of the 1st century A.D, affirms a Lucianic LXX text as part of the standard Old Testament uncorrupted at the time when scholars say the present Masoretic was newly made the standard. They will conclude Josephus' mixed text was just an "evolution leftover." But believing in inerrancy, and believing that Josephus knew more about text history than modern scholars do, we conclude something very different, that at this time in history, many Hellenist Jews still adhered to a receding earlier tradition of an LXX text that amplified the standard Masoretic, along with a Masoretic standard. The Lucianic LXX would still be perceived by many Hellenist Jews as a product of providential progression of revelation, a perception continuing from the Aristeus letter writer and Philo. This tradition evidently was not yet excluded by a providential Masoretic-conformity trend.

But rapid change was in the wind after destruction of the second temple in 70 A.D. when Jews began to abandon writings of LXX defenders, and the Pharisaic movement neared its goal of ending competition with the Masoretic standard. Not long after Josephus' writing, the Jewish attitude in the matter was reversed. The amplified genuine LXX text of Josephus and its Hebrew basis passed into textual oblivion to prevent competition with a now fully-unveiled Bible text. This would be finalized on completion of the New Testament with the Revelation book at ~100 A.D. At this time preservation of LXX amplification in the New Testament would conclude preservation of amplification begun long ago in mild form in early standard-text books and continuing in pre-exilic and post-exilic books.

That Josephus' Lucianic LXX was based on a providentially-pure Hebrew text is attested in that he never quoted apocrypha as scripture, while all extant LXX forms include apocrypha as part of the scripture text. Philo referred to the Lucianic LXX, not mentioning apocrypha, the Pentateuch being his only apparent interest. Thus the earliest revered LXX likely was a Lucianic-type text without apocrypha. Apocrypha would begin to enter the LXX text in minor degree in the 2nd-1st centuries B.C, not being widely accepted until the early church era when some churches advocated them. In the absence of apocrypha, the claim for Lucianic-text originality is further strengthened against any such claim for Vaticanus.

The "Silent" Period between the Testaments

It is said that the long period between the late 5th - century B.C. final Old Testament book and the Advent of Christ was a period of ~400 years of silence in which God spoke nothing to His people. But from our discussion of amplification, we might see this period as continuing the ancient unveiling of God's Word, revealing a unique amplified Old Testament in the 3rd-2nd century Lucianic LXX that continued earlier less-advanced amplification in the 6th-5th century post-exilic standard-text books. Thus the original Christological LXX would have been a forerunner that announced the coming of Christ and the church era.

Perhaps in post-exilic books of the late 6th - late 5th centuries B.C, God gave major amplification of vital past history so that His people might avoid past failure and seek new consecrated service. As failure continued, prophetic books of Zechariah, Malachi and Haggai penned in this period heralded the future Messiah's offer of righteousness to God's people, despite past and ongoing failures. Thus we see a 3rd-2nd century B.C. original Lucianic LXX, without apocrypha, as a providential review of Old Testament history, an unveiled final look at everything in which God's people failed, and revealing in final clarity, Messiah as their one hope for the future. Accordingly, we view the New Testament of Messiah, linked to its Old Testament foundation through the Lucianic original LXX, as the ultimate guide for God's people, showing the way of ultimate righteousness. In this we see all self-effort in obedience to God's holy law failing in finality and superseded in Christ Jesus, the long-awaited Hope of Israel and the Savior of the world. He gives the salvation power by which the spirit of the holy law is fulfilled in all His people.

Epilogue: Scripture in the Contemporary World

If we trust God to preserve His Word for His people, we find it in the living tradition of His people doing His work. Aberrant discarded texts, likely associated with a cult, can't represent the scripture diet of the entire Judaic culture. Literary appetites of an isolated aberrant sect don't compare with the Masoretic Text of martyr-like Jewish scribes who devoted their lives to preserve the true standard text, one so sacred to them they would destroy the laborious work, or bury it in a geniza to ensure against its desecration, and they would discard competing distorted texts to eliminate competition with the true one. The great potential for error in texts discarded in caves and archives, is seen in the error of modern scholars who exalt such texts. A rare providence has revealed the true antiquity of the Masoretic-Text history, yet scholars dwell on aberrant texts and find little of interest in the message of standard-text antiquity. The finding of true canonical texts at Wadi Murabbaat, Masada, and even Qumran, offers clues that Providence has put in our path for edification. But scholars keep imagining text history based on evolution theory of dead secularism. Association of the name Dead Sea with the scrolls seems to mock scholar interest in dead things.

May all who love the appearing of the Living Word, forsake husks exhumed from graves and exalt His living written Word.

Topic C End Notes

1. Cross, F.M. 1992. "The Text Behind the Text of the Hebrew Bible." *Understanding the Dead Sea Scrolls.* Ed. by H. Shanks. N.Y. Random House. p145-146

2. Schiffman, L.H. 1994. *Reclaiming the Dead Sea Scrolls.* Phila. The Jewish Publication Society. p169-180

3. Roberts, B.J. 1969. "The Old Testament: Manuscripts, Text and Versions." *The Cambridge History of the Bible.* Ed. G.W.H. Lampe. Cambridge Univ. Press. p1-26

4. Gordon, R.P. 1986. "The Ancient Versions." *The International Bible Com.* ed. F.F. Bruce. N.Y. Guideposts. p15

5. *Davis Dictionary of the Bible.* 1973. Nashville. Royal. p711

6. Cross, F.M. 1975. "Evolution of a Theory of Local Texts." *Qumran and the History of the Biblical Text.* ed. F.M. Cross & S. Talmon. Cambridge. Harvard Press. p177- 95

7. Cross, Op.Cit. p306-315

8. VanderKam, J.C. 1994. *The Dead Sea Scrolls Today.* Grand Rapids. Eerdmans. p 133

9. Sanderson, J.E. 1986. *An Exodus Scroll from Qumran: 4Q Paleo-Exodm.* Atlanta. Scholars Press. p17-28

10. Golb, N. 1995. *Who Wrote the Dead Sea Scrolls?* N.Y. Scribner. p117-150

11. VanderKam. Op. Cit p30-32

12. Skehan, P.W. Qumran and the History of the Biblical Text. p266

13. Eisenman, R.H. & Wise, M. 1992. "The Dead Sea Scrolls Uncovered." Rockport, MS. Element Inc. p75-77

14. Van Der Kooij, A. 1990."The Old Greek of Isaiah in Relation to the Qumran Texts of Isaiah." *LXX: Septuagint, Scrolls and Cognate Writings.* ed. G.F. Brooke & B. Lindars. Atlanta. Scholars Press. p195-209

15. Mansoor, M. 1964. *The Dead Sea Scrolls.* Grand Rapids. Eerdmans. p75

16. Talmon, S. Op. Cit. *Qumran and the History of the Biblical Text.* p 32

17. Brownlee, W.H. 1964. *The Meaning of the Qumran Scrolls for the Bible.* N.Y. Oxford Univ. Press. p46

18. Schiffman. Op. Cit. p181-195

19. Grabbe, L.L. Op. Cit. *LXX: Septuagint, Scrolls and Cognate Writings.* p505-517

20. O' Connell, K.G. 1972. *The Theodotionic Revision of the Book of Exodus.* Cambridge, Ma. Harvard U. Press. p293

21. Kahle, P.E. 1959. *The Cairo Geniza.* Oxford. Basil Blackwell. p 218-232

22. Tov, E. Op. Cit. *Qumran and the History of the Biblical Text* p 293-302.

23. Jellicoe, S. 1968. *The Septuagint and Modern Study.* Oxford at the Clarendon Press. p243-268

24. Ulrich, E.C. 1978. *The Qumran Text of Samuel and Josep*hus. Missoula, Mt. Scholars Press. p15-37

25. De Waard, J. 1966. *A Comparative Study of the Old Testament Text in the Dead Sea Scrolls and in the New Testament.* Leiden. E.J. Brill. p15

26. Jellicoe. Op. Cit. p157

27. Ewert, D. 1983. *From Ancient Tablets to Modern Translations.* Grand Rapids. Zondervan. p70

Brief Glossary

Amplification: The advancing or clarifying of the text teaching in an earlier Old Testament book by a later book or by the New Testament.

Consonantal text: A text with consonants, but no vowels.

Lucianic LXX: A Septuagint text that appears to best represent an original inerrant text, and is quite different from that based largely on corrupt Vaticanus and Sinaiticus manuscripts.

Ketiv: The text proper in the Old Testament.

Matres Lectionis: Consonants serving double duty as vowels.

Pointing: A system of signs inserted above and below consonants to signify vowels and enable consistent pronunciation.

Qere: Margin notes commenting on the text, most being added by the Masoretes in the Middle Ages, but certain ancient ones originating in the text before the canon closed.

Qumran The name of the location in the Dead Sea region where the Dead-Sea scrolls were found.

Samaritan Pentateuch: A copy of the Hebrew Pentateuch that is the property of the Samaritans and not much different basically from the Masoretic-Text Pentateuch, the important difference being certain modifications that reflect Samaritan dogma.

Septuagint: Greek translation of the Hebrew text, also called the LXX (referring to 70 translators). The Lucianic form is more accurate than much-corrupted ones in 4th-5th century manuscripts Vaticanus, Sinaiticus and Alexandrinus.

Targumim: Aramaic-language translations of the Hebrew that paraphrase to an extent and serve as commentary to an extent.

Lightning Source UK Ltd.
Milton Keynes UK
UKOW05f1834210417
299663UK00007B/377/P